Sacred Echoes of Faith

Sacred Echoes of Faith

A PRIEST'S EXPLORATION OF THE DIVINE GUIDANCE RECEIVED THROUGH LETTER WRITING

FATHER TOM HERON

Copyright © 2025 Father Tom Heron,

eleven twenty-four Productions, LLC

ISBN 978-1-7364750-5-8

All Rights Reserved, including the right to reproduce this book or portions thereof in any form whatsoever. This work is copyrighted by the publisher. No unauthorized duplication or presentation allowed. Reviewers may quote small portions for the sake of review written for inclusion in a magazine, newspaper, or journal; however, expressed, written permission by the publisher is required prior to publication.

For information about special discounts for bulk purchases, please contact the publisher at eleven24sales@gmail.com

Version 1

Because of the dynamic nature of the internet, any web addresses or links contained in this book may have changed since the publication and may no longer be valid.

All names, images, and/or likenesses contained herein have given verbal and/or written permission to the author to be included. Some names have been changed or omitted to protect the privacy of the individuals.

All biblical citations included in this work have been sourced from the New American Bible (Revised Edition), also known as NABRE, unless otherwise noted in the text.

I dedicate this book to my favorite and best college professor, Monsignor Francis Carbine, who inspired me to value the gift of words, written and spoken. For more than fifty years, he encouraged and challenged me to become a better writer, a better person, and a better priest. I am forever indebted to him and grateful for his lasting impact on my life.

In loving memory of Margaret M. (Dyer) Burghart

December 11, 1952 – May 22, 2025

Contents

Foreword

BY KEVIN HASLAM

There are moments in life when certain people walk into your world at exactly the right time, as if nudged by something greater than coincidence. For me, Father Tom Heron is one of those people. I first met him in 2016, during a chapter of my life that felt unmoored. I'd just moved into a community near St. Matthew's Parish, freshly navigating the emotional aftermath of a few major life changes. I was searching … for purpose, for belonging, for a spark to reignite my faith.

What began as a practical appointment to discuss becoming a godfather to my dear friends' firstborn child transformed into a conversation that would change both of our lives.

I entered that rectory with nothing but questions, uncertainties, and an offer to donate my time, because at the time, money was something I couldn't afford to give.

From the moment we started talking, Father Tom and I clicked. Maybe it was our shared love of Philadelphia sports and physical fitness, or maybe it was his unique ability to make you feel seen and understood, as if your story genuinely mattered. When I casually mentioned that I'd written a book a couple of years earlier, his eyes lit up. He shared his own dream of publishing a book, a dream that had stalled twice before. I can still see his smile when he looked me in the eye that day. I can still hear his words echoing in my mind, "Maybe third time's the charm!"

That simple, hopeful statement sparked a journey that has now spanned three books, countless conversations, and an enduring partnership, along with his dear friend Mary Kay, rooted in trust and faith.

I left the rectory that day having begun a friendship that has truly made me a better man … the man I am today some eight years later.

Father Tom's first book, *We Are All Called,* was his memoir, but more importantly a passionate tale of growing through the weeds and wheat of his calling to be a priest. His second, *An Introductory Guide to Spiritual Maturity,* offered a roadmap for growing in faith through bite-sized reflections—the kind of wisdom you could turn to at the end of a long day, like a well-worn nightstand book. Now, with *Sacred Echoes of Faith,* Father Tom calls us into something both timeless and timely: the art of letter writing as a path to deepening faith.

In a world consumed by the speed of texts and the brevity of social media posts, letter writing feels almost antiquated. It demands intention. It asks us to slow down, to reflect, to offer a piece of ourselves through well-thought-out words. Father Tom's letters are more than just words on paper; they are windows into his soul, testaments to his authenticity, vulnerability, and intense belief in the power of human and divine interaction.

And that is one of the most striking aspects of this book: its raw honesty. Father Tom doesn't shy away from the difficult topics or the imperfections of his own humanity. He doesn't write to portray himself as someone perfect or holier-than-thou. He writes *and lives* as someone who puts his pants on one leg at a time (as he often says); as someone who wrestles with the same questions and struggles that we all face. He writes with courage, addressing conflict, expressing opinions in a divided world, and confronting the messy realities of life with the echo of the Gospel.

What makes *Sacred Echoes of Faith* so compelling is that it's not just a book for one generation or one type of reader. While those who grew up in the era of handwritten letters may find it nostalgic and relatable, it's also a challenge to younger generations to rediscover the depth and intimacy that comes from slowing down and putting pen to paper. This book is an invitation—to write, to reflect, to connect, and to see how the simple act of writing a letter can become an act of faith.

As someone who's had the privilege of working alongside Father Tom on this project, I can tell you this: Every word in these pages comes from a place of genuine love and intention. He writes with the kind of authenticity that makes you want to sit down and write a letter of your own—to a loved one, to a friend, or even to God Himself. He reminds us that in the act of writing, we not only connect with others but also come to know ourselves more deeply. And in knowing ourselves, we come closer to knowing the One who created us.

Father Tom's resilience shines brightly in these pages. Despite health challenges and personal losses in recent years, his spirit remains unyielding, his love for writing undimmed. This book combines the two greatest elements from his first two: It is, in many ways, both a love story and a guide. It's a love story with authenticity and self-discovery, and it's a guide to growing closer to divine love by first growing closer to ourselves and one another.

It's been an honor to walk alongside Father Tom on this journey and to witness the evolution of his voice and vision over the past eight years. I highly recommend this book to anyone because in a world spinning in haste, *Sacred Echoes of Faith* invites us to pause, to reflect, and to let our faith echo through the written word.

So, grab a pen. Open your heart. And let this book remind you of the sacredness in every letter, every connection, every echo of faith.

Kevin Haslam
Owner + Publisher, eleven24

Preface

THE LETTERS THAT BIND US

Why write a book on letters? In this fast-paced world where digital snippets dominate communication and "280 characters" are the norm, letters stand as a quiet, enduring testament to something more intense: connection, reflection, and the divine echoes of faith. My third book, *Sacred Echoes of Faith,* is not merely a collection of thoughts; it is a journey into the art of letter writing, a journey I've been blessed to embark upon throughout my vocation as a priest.

Jesus instructs his disciples—his lifelong students—to bring "from his storeroom both the new and the old" (Matthew 13:52). There is no doubt in my mind that I have an old soul. That is to say, I prefer letter-writing to texting.

Letter writing holds a special place in the fabric of human history, and its roots are deeply spiritual. The Apostle Paul's epistles built up the early Church, bridging physical distances to foster spiritual growth. Letters inspire, console, and bring distant souls close. When written prayerfully, they allow the writer and the recipient to meet the Blessed Trinity in the sacred space of words. In my own life, writing letters has been both an extension of ministry and a reflection of my spiritual journey.

The impetus for this book came unexpectedly. My very good friend Bill Mattia of 55 years nudged me to consider the power of letter writing, planting the seed for this endeavor. Over the decades, I have exchanged letters with parishioners, friends, and fellow clergy, not to mention letters to the editor and even the leaders of our country and our church! Each letter has become a thread in the tapestry of faith and community. From humorous exchanges to heartfelt condolences, these letters are a record of shared moments, a window into the joys and struggles of discipleship.

Looking back, I realize that this book is an outgrowth of my earlier works. *We Are All Called* explored the births we encounter on our spiritual journeys: natural, spiritual, vocational, and eternal. *An Introductory Guide to Spiritual Maturity* focused on growing in holiness through the liturgical seasons. In this third endeavor, I aim to show how letter writing can guide us to even greater spiritual maturity and divine connection.

So, the question remains: Why letters? They demand something rare in today's culture: intentionality. Writing a letter is a sacred act of slowing down, of reflecting deeply on another person's life and one's own life, especially for people who journal. Unlike hurried text messages or emails, letters require the writer to pause, to pray, and to pour out their heart. The result is not just a piece of paper but an enduring gift—a testimony of faith and love that carries the echoes of divine presence.

My first mentor, Monsignor Dan Murray, was instrumental in teaching me the art of spiritual direction and, indirectly, the art of letter writing. In my seminary years, he encouraged me to record my thoughts and experiences. "You must write," he would say after hearing me recount a story from ministry or a pastoral encounter. It was not just advice. It was a summons to see divinity in everyday life and to share that vision with others.

BLESSED ARE THE CLEAN OF HEART, FOR THEY WILL SEE GOD. (MATTHEW 5:8)

Dan's encouragement marked the beginning of my habit of capturing life through letters. That tender touch of a spiritual director gave me the confidence I needed to explore my writing. Because when you're convinced that you're loved, fear, doubt, and suffering all make sense. When you're not convinced that you're loved, you get too often overwhelmed by fear and doubt, and you try to avoid suffering at all costs. A mature disciple of Jesus recognizes that joy and suffering can coexist. You have to have a long, deep, daily loving relationship with Father, Son, and Holy Spirit. If you read the Gospels over and over again, they're almost intertwined. You can have peace, hope, and joy with hardship, difficulty, and suffering, but the key is that you have to grow in spiritual maturity to make that revelation.

For example, one woman wanted me to bless her marriage after her husband died. Sacraments are for the living, and he died during Ash Wednesday. She asked me to put ashes on his head. Wild stories like that, where faith and despair intermingle, can often become humorous upon reflection through writing. Other times, we must grieve with our Christian comrades, and I never skip the practice of writing letters of consolation to reach grieving families. These writings became a ministry in themselves. They allowed me to extend the sacraments, to offer grace where it was most needed, even from a distance.

But Dan's influence went deeper. He believed in discipline and clarity in writing. "You have a long way to go," he would often say, pushing me to refine my craft. His death left an ache in my heart but also a resolve to continue the mission he started. This book is, in part, a tribute to his mentorship.

This work also reflects my journey of self-discovery, and there were other mentors, too. Early in my life, mentors like my high school English teacher, Jim McGrath, and seminary professor, Father Fran Carbine, encouraged my love for writing. Their critiques humbled me, their praise spurred me forward. They showed me that writing is both a gift and a discipline, a way to wrestle with God's call and to communicate His truth.

Father Carbine, tough as nails, particularly took me under his wing as my English teacher. He was known for giving two grades: one for content and one for style. A "5" was the best you could get in either category, and no one got a "5/5" in Carbine's class. He always found that missing comma to knock it down a notch. Yet, his style was helpful in a way to humble a young, egotistical mind.

May 14, 2002

Reverend Thomas J. Heron

Dear Tom,

As I read your personal **Odyssey** in today's **Inquirer**, I thought of the line in St. Jessica Powers' poem, "Gaelic Music" : "I run with it, away from commonplaces/ from ditto marks called days and frequent faces."

Your world is hardly one of ditto days! Your "postage stamp of earth" seems to be cobbled together with themes from Poe, the dark sonnets of G.M. Hopkins, Samuel Beckett with a bit of Kafka thrown in to lighten the mood. These men likewise steered clear of "commonplaces."

While I am impressed by your fondness for Juvenal, I was disappointed by your failure to give homage to Joseph Conrad who described our world as a "raging, blind darkness that howled, and where man can only give back 'yell' for 'yell.'"

Thank God for your commitment to endorphins and elan - ingredients in the Heronian "yell"!

Jessica Powers, a Carmelite Sister, is well worth knowing. She writes of "a city estranged from every bird and butterfly." At the same time, in "The Mystical Sparrow of St. John of the Cross" she describes the "mystical sparrow" as it "sings in jubilation/ alone upon the housetop of creation."

Maybe your present calling is to be like Power's Abraham, "that old weather-beaten unwavering nomad" asking about the mileage between Ur and Haran.

What the Aegean was to Odysseus, Hibbard's Stadium & Good Shepherd (with its dudes and "pay to play" ladies) are to yourself. These days, your challenges may not all be vertical, but you seem to be top of them all.... maybe like the "mystical sparrow."

Here in my own Yoknapatawpha and with Hibernian (i.e. Ulster) Regards I remain

Cordially yours,

Fran Carbine

Father Fran Carbine's critique of my letter written to the Philadelphia Inquirer in 2002.

Over the years, writing letters became a bridge to my parishioners and friends. It allowed me to accompany them in their joys and sorrows. Whether it was a thank-you note, a letter of recommendation, or a message of encouragement, these letters deepened relationships and anchored me more firmly in my vocation. Each letter reminded me that I am not merely a shepherd but also a fellow pilgrim, navigating the same spiritual terrain as those I serve.

As I sit down to write this book, I am mindful of its purpose. It is not just a collection of letters; it is an invitation to rediscover the lost art of writing as a spiritual practice. I hope to show how letters can be a source of healing, guidance, and connection. In a world that often feels fragmented, these writings can knit us together, reflecting the unity we share in Christ.

Every letter I have written bears the marks of grace, the fingerprints of Father, Son, and Holy Spirit, who work through our human words and gestures. It is my desire for this book to inspire others to pick up a pen, to open their hearts, and to let their faith resonate through the written word. For in writing, we not only express ourselves, we echo the divine.

May this work serve as a testament to the power of letters to transform, to console, and to lead us closer to the One who first wrote His law on our hearts. With gratitude and hope, I invite you to join me in this exploration of sacred correspondence.

Introduction

GRACE IN EVERY LETTER

In today's world, something profound is slipping through the cracks. We live in an age where we are inundated with means of connection but often fail to truly connect. In the race to communicate faster, we have lost the depth and substance that make human interaction meaningful. This is where the art of letter writing becomes not just a nostalgic relic but a spiritual act, a lifeline to clarity, connection, and communion.

We live in a crazy paradox when it comes to communication. There are more and more means of communicating with one another, yet less communication overall. What a tragedy!

A letter, unlike its fleeting digital counterparts, is tangible. It carries the weight of intention. To write a letter is to slow down, to consider the recipient's life as well as your own, and to offer a part of yourself through words. Letters avoid the pitfalls of modern communication—missed calls, misinterpreted texts, and the sense of hurried detachment. When you open a letter, it invites the presence of the sender into the room. The ink on the page is a physical extension of the hand that wrote it, making the words feel alive. This is why so many of us hold onto letters long after their words have been read. They become sacred moments of "holy communion."

There is something deeply human and intensely divine about this kind of communication. It transcends time and space, as we see in Sacred Scripture. The New Testament is filled with letters; fourteen of them attributed to St. Paul alone. These epistles were not just theological dissertations; they were lifelines to fledgling Christian communities. In his letters, Paul greeted his readers warmly, addressed their concerns candidly, and left them with words of encouragement that still resonate today. He understood that letters could clarify misunderstandings, offer correction, and build unity. They were not simply messages; they were instruments of spiritual transformation.

St. John, the beloved disciple, wrote his letters decades after walking with Jesus. In one of them, he distilled the Gospel to its most essential truth: "God is love." That simple phrase holds an entire world of meaning, one that letter writing invites us to explore in the quiet reflection of ink on paper.

But letters are more than a tool for sharing theological truths; they are a means of connecting human experience to the divine. Consider the story of John Lennon's piano, the instrument on which he composed *Imagine*. After Lennon's tragic death, the piano became a curio of sorts. Decades later, it traveled the world as fans lined up to see it as if the piano carried his presence, as if his creative essence lingered in its keys.[1] Similarly, a letter carries the presence of the writer. It becomes a vessel through which the writer's thoughts, feelings, and even spirit can touch the recipient. This is especially true in spiritual life, where words can become a conduit for grace, healing, and encouragement.

As a priest, one of my primary tasks is to assure people of God's loving presence in their lives. Remember, when a person is convinced that he or she is loved, that person lives his or her life differently. They live life freely and abundantly. That is the "way" Jesus wants us to live every day. Fear, doubt, and suffering often create a sense of isolation, but the spiritual life is a journey into the Paschal Mystery: the birth, life, suffering, death, and resurrection of Jesus Christ. Letters can serve as guideposts on this journey, helping others navigate the joys and trials of discipleship. A thoughtfully written letter can nudge someone toward understanding the difference between suffering rooted in love and suffering born of sin, violence, or hatred. We live in a culture that tries to avoid and eliminate pain as quickly as possible and at all costs. That letter you write to a friend in need can offer a word of hope, reminding them that they are not alone in their struggles.

The act of writing a letter mirrors the act of prayer. Both require time, attention, and vulnerability. Both seek to bridge the gap between oneself and another, be it another person or the three divine persons of Father, Son, and Holy Spirit.

In thc Creed that we pray, "...we believe in things visible and invisible..." This is an attempt to bring divine order out of the abstract and into the daily concreteness of your life. Every morning when I wake up, the first thing I say is, "God, come to my assistance, make haste to help me," because I do have a strong relationship with Father, Son, and Holy Spirit. I don't know what the day is going to bring, but if I have divine assistance, I'm not taking on the day alone. The next thing I pray is, "This is the day you have made, and I rejoice, and I am glad that you gave me another day."

When I write a letter, I often include cartoons or inspiring quotes to bring laughter and lightheartedness, followed by words of encouragement to uplift the spirit. These small gestures are not trivial; they reflect the humanity and love that undergird our relationships. As Leon Bloy famously wrote, "The only real sadness, the only real failure, the only great tragedy in life, is not to become a saint."[2] Sometimes, all it takes is a well-timed word to set someone on the path to sanctity.

Letter writing, like all meaningful communication, requires revision. It demands thoughtfulness and the discipline to refine our words. Unlike a hastily spoken comment or a curt text, a letter allows the writer to clarify their thoughts to ensure that what is expressed is true and kind. This discipline, in turn, fosters spiritual growth as it calls us to examine our own hearts and intentions.

Throughout this book, we will explore the many dimensions of letter writing—its capacity to connect individuals, its potential to deepen our relationship with the divine, and its role as a tool for reflection and healing. We will journey through the therapeutic aspects of writing, the joy of sharing lighthearted moments, and the wholehearted sense of connection that comes from meaningful correspondence. We will also explore the more challenging aspects of writing, such as expressing an opinion on a controversial topic or dealing with a conflict in the workplace. From thank-you notes to letters of consolation, each chapter will consider a different facet of this sacred art. The letters you will read that I have written are raw and unadulterated. They are true to my core being.

And for the letters you will read that were addressed to me, they are unedited and captured in that moment in time. Some senders' and recipients' names have been changed or omitted to protect their identities. Others have granted me permission to use their writing with attribution.

We will also draw inspiration from Scripture, where letters played a pivotal role in the growth of the early Church. Paul sent his good friend Timothy to the city of Ephesus[3], and his good friend Titus to the city of Crete[4]. He and Barnabas got along well, but they had a falling out.[5] Not only did he send letters, but he also sent flesh and blood believers to try to sustain a community and keep it on the right track to avoid heresy. The Acts of the Apostles is really a letter that St. Luke wrote on expanding this sect of Judeo-Christianity into the world of the Gentiles. Letter writing should expand our horizons, open us up ... That's what those letters are really trying to do ... to clarify the truth. Their letters remind us that true communication is not a one-sided affair; it is a reciprocal exchange that enriches both the sender and the recipient.

So, as we embark on this exploration together, I invite you to reflect on your own experiences with letter writing. Who has written to you in a way that touched your soul? Whose life might you touch with your words? Letters have the power to transform not only relationships but also the human heart. They invite us to move beyond the superficial into the realm of the substantive, where true connection and meaning are found.

In the next chapter, we'll begin with the basics: how simple acts like thank-you notes and letters of recommendation can become sincere expressions of faith and love. For now, let us pause and consider the gift of the written word and how, like the disciples of old, we too are called to carry the message of love and grace to the ends of the Earth.

CHAPTER 1

Pen and Paper as Needle and Thread

WEAVING PAST, PRESENT, AND FUTURE THROUGH LETTER-WRITING BASICS

In my childhood home, gratitude wasn't just taught, it was expected. My mother had a way of instilling it into us like a foundational virtue, something that defined who we were and how we treated others. As a young boy, I learned this lesson one handwritten thank-you note at a time.

My mom, who had to be both mother and father after my dad's early death, was firm but loving. She would say, "Tom, you have to write a thank-you note as soon as you get a gift. Don't let it sit." I must have been seven years old when she sat me at the kitchen table with a stack of cards, instructing me to name the gift specifically, write neatly, and do it with genuine thoughtfulness. This wasn't a throwaway task; it was a sacred obligation to acknowledge kindness and express appreciation.

Once I finished a note, she would read it with an eagle eye, inspecting every line. If I had written "Thank you for your gift" without mentioning exactly what the gift was, back to the table I went. "You can't just say thank you. That says nothing. Be specific, Tom. Let them know you noticed." If an aunt sent me

$5, I had to write, "Thank you for the $5. I'm going to use it to buy a new baseball glove."

February 28, 2022

Dear Mary,

Charity is the signature of every saint! Thank you for the two Fifty Dollar Giant Gift Cards. I am grateful to you for being so generous to me. May the Lord reward you a hundred-fold.

Gratitude engenders other virtues such as generosity, humility, compassion, wisdom, joy, integrity and trust. The daily practice of gratitude keeps the heart open regardless of what comes our way. The disposition of mindfulness, of being aware of and thankful for our blessings, helps cultivate our virtues and significantly diminishes or can even eradicate any obstacles to gratitude we may face.

"If you concentrate on finding whatever is good in every situation, you will discover that your life will suddenly be filled with gratitude, a feeling that nurtures the soul."

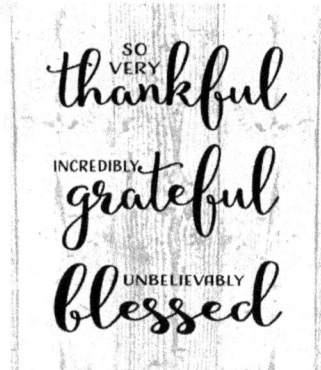

Love,

Tom

SO VERY

INCREDIBLY

UNBELIEVABLY
blessed

An example of a thank-you letter in response to a gift I received; an artful craft, to say the least!

Woe to my brother, who was always in a rush. My mother would laugh about his sloppiness, but her lesson was clear: Gratitude must be timely, sincere, and specific. Send it quickly. Don't wait six months, or people won't even remember what they gave you. My mother's insistence was rooted in her understanding of the human condition: A gift deserves recognition, and a person deserves to know that their kindness matters.

I've carried her lesson with me my entire life. I can still hear her voice saying, "If you lose your sense of gratitude, you become an impoverished person." Will Rogers put it beautifully: "You'll never meet a happy person who isn't grateful." That is as true today as it was then.

ACKNOWLEDGING THE PAST IN THE GRACIOUS PRESENT

In the late 1950s and early 60s, thank-you notes and handwritten letters were commonplace. Gratitude was not just a sentiment; it was a discipline, something you practiced as naturally as breathing. Today, that discipline has faded. If you receive a response at all, it's likely to be a quick text message or an email filled with emojis ... a thumbs-up 👍, a smiley face 🙂, a few exclamation points!!!

Don't get me wrong, technology has its place. But there's something deeply artificial about the speed and brevity of modern communication. A text message arrives in an instant, jolting you with its immediacy. You respond in kind, almost reflexively, without much thought. A letter, on the other hand, requires patience. It demands reflection. It moves against the grain of our bite-sized world, reclaiming the time and space needed to make a genuine connection. There is no "undo" button after the mail carrier removes it from your mailbox!

And now, with artificial intelligence, you can even outsource your thank-you notes. You type in a few keywords, and the program generates a note for you. But what is lost in that process? The soul of the writer. The sincerity of their voice. The warmth of their personality. A thank-you written by a machine says nothing about the human connection that prompted it. A handwritten letter is different. It carries your thoughts, your intentions, and your humanity.

A thank-you letter may seem like the simplest form of communication, but it carries extraordinary weight. It affirms the goodness of the giver, strengthens the bond between two people, and enriches the writer. Gratitude, when expressed with thought and care, deepens the human experience. It lifts us out of our self-absorption and makes us more aware of the beauty of others' generosity.

Thank-you letters don't need to be long or elaborate, but they do need to be thoughtful. When I was ten years old, my uncle took me to my first Phillies game. I can still remember the magic of that night. Connie Mack Stadium lit up like a cathedral, the vivid green of the grass under the lights, the thrill of opening day against the Reds. It wasn't just a baseball game; it was an experience that stayed with me for years. My uncle may have paid for the ticket, but he gave me something far more valuable: a memory. That's what I wrote to him in my thank-you note. I told him what I loved most about that night and how much it meant to spend time with him. He knew from my words that his gift had made a difference.

Dear Ellie,

Thank you for lunch at Outback today. The meal was delicious. The company was grace. I am pleased to have met your life-long friend Rose.

Thanks also for the cross with the Blessed Sacrament. The two foundations of our Catholic faith. I am grateful to you for your lively faith and generosity. Lastly, thanks for the black bag—better than pink.

Sincerely in Our Lord,

Fr. Tom

Fr. Tom Heron

Not just a letter of thanks, but a "thinking of our experience together," as grace can be found in life's every moment.

A thank-you note doesn't have to be perfect. But it must be intentional. The same is true in our spiritual lives. The Psalms remind us time and again to give thanks.

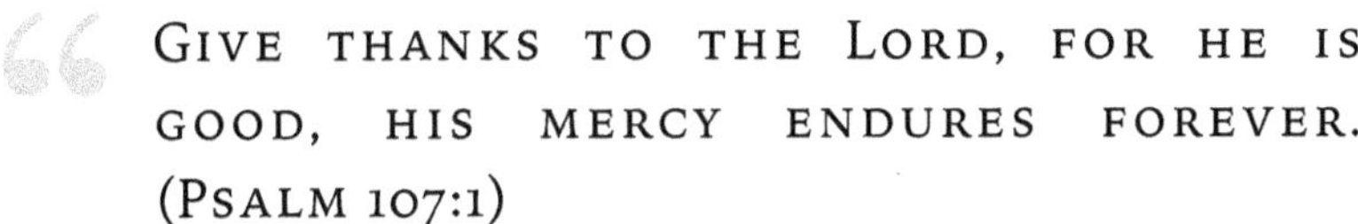

> GIVE THANKS TO THE LORD, FOR HE IS GOOD, HIS MERCY ENDURES FOREVER. (PSALM 107:1)

Gratitude is a spiritual posture. It humbles us, centers us, and draws us closer to God and others. It softens our hearts when we give glory to God, and for that, I pray, "Holy Spirit, let words of gratitude be always on my lips (and in my written word)."

It's worth noting that a thank-you letter doesn't just benefit the recipient. It also transforms the writer. When someone gives you a gift, their kindness pushes you to dig deeper into your own heart to discover the words that will match their generosity. In finding the words, you uncover something more: an appreciation for the interconnectedness of life and love. That journey of writing creates meaning.

THE ART OF INFLUENCE OVER A BETTER FUTURE

If thank-you letters look back, letters of recommendation look forward. They advocate for someone's future, offering the reader a glimpse into their character, abilities, and potential.

I remember the first time I needed a letter of recommendation for myself. I was applying to college, and my high school teachers graciously wrote on my behalf. At the time, I didn't fully appreciate what those letters meant. I just hoped they were good enough to get me where I needed to go. But as I got older, I realized what a gift it is to have someone put their own name on the line for you, to write words that vouch for your character.

October 23, 2002

Office of Continuing Education
Saint Meinrad School of Theology
St. Meinrad, IN 47577

Dear Sir/Madam:

I am writing this letter of reference on behalf of Father J. Thomas Heron who is applying for admission to your Office of Continuing Education/Sabbatical Program.

I have known Father Heron since 1970 when he entered Saint Charles Borromeo Seminary where I was Professor of Sacred Scripture. I have been his spiritual director from that time to the present. Father Heron is an excellent student, well read, and deeply spiritual. In his priestly ministry for these past 24 plus years he has shown the face of Christ to people of all ages and all economic backgrounds. In his present position as Pastor of Good Shepherd Parish he has exhibited heroic virtue in the face of a deteriorating cultural situation. I might add that in my position as Rector of Saint Charles Borromeo Seminary I asked him to serve on our Formation Committee where he was instrumental for seven years in putting together an excellent curriculum especially on celibacy.

I recommend him to you without any reservation.

Sincerely yours,

Daniel A. Murray

Rev. Msgr. Daniel A. Murray, S.T.L., S.S.L.

My spiritual director, Monsignor Dan Murray, had a way with words. Here is one of his kindest testimonials for me. A great honor.

Years later, my mentor, Monsignor Dan Murray, wrote a recommendation for me to attend a prestigious theology program. I read it and realized how well he understood me—not just what I had accomplished but what I aspired to become. A good letter of recommendation doesn't simply list a person's qualifications; it shines a light on who they are and who they can be.

January 9, 2013

Admissions Office

To Whom It May Concern:

I am writing on behalf of is presently a senior at Cardinal O'Hara High School and a member of St. Pius X Parish. My association with began four years ago when was in 8th grade. In this time I have enjoyed contact with him and his family.

has many solid personal traits. He is reliable, dependable and responsible. He is friendly and has the ability to think clearly when an emergency arises. demonstrates a willingness to learn and takes initiative when appropriate. He is blessed with a wonderful sense of humor.

I recommend without reservation to continue his education at the

If you need more information do not hesitate to contact me at the above address.

Sincerely in Our Lord,

Fr. Tom

Fr. Tom Heron

But one example of how I thoughtfully and seriously write a letter of recommendation.

When someone asks me to write a letter of recommendation today, I don't take it lightly. I want to know their story more than just their resume. "Tell me why this opportunity matters to you," I'll say. "Help me understand what makes you the right person for it." A recommendation letter, when done right, can open doors for someone. But it's not just about securing an opportunity. It's about affirming the person's worth, potential, and dignity.

TO ACKNOWLEDGE TRAGEDY IS ONE SMALL ATTEMPT AT MAKING LIFE ANEW

Thank-you letters and recommendation letters are often joyful exchanges. But some letters must confront the most difficult human experiences: sickness, grief, and loss. These are the letters that demand the most from us as writers because they require vulnerability, courage, and love.

JOANNE CAMPION Rec'd 8/20/23

Dear Father,
Thank you for all
your prayers during Dicks
illness. They were such a
comfort to him and me. And
thank you for saying his Mass
tomorrow. God Bless you
Joanne

"Dear Father, Thank you for all your prayers during Dick's illness. They were such a comfort to him and me. And thank you for saying his Mass tomorrow. God bless you, Joanne"

When a loved one dies, words often fail. And yet, it is in these moments of pain that a letter can become a balm for the soul. I have written countless letters to grieving families, offering words of consolation rooted in faith. I often turn to the Book of Wisdom.

> THE SOULS OF THE RIGHTEOUS ARE IN THE HAND OF GOD, AND NO TORMENT SHALL TOUCH THEM. (WISDOM 3:1)

Scripture speaks to the depth of human sadness in a way that our own words often cannot. But even so, a letter—no matter how imperfect—can remind a grieving person that they are not alone, and writing a letter of their own can help them process and reflect in a healthy, spiritual way.

November 1, 2022

Dr. Bradley Wasserman

Dear Dr. Wasserman,

"Give thanks to the Lord for he is good." Psalm 118

You have performed a medical miracle and Lazarus-like resurrection for me as your patient since October 17, 2022.

The Regenokine treatment of several injections on five different days has freed me from massive inflammation, crushing fatigue, significant suffering and distress, as well as physical weakness which I experienced since December 13, 2021 up to November 2, 2022 that was triggered by the Covid booster shot.

I am forever grateful to you for being a compassionate doctor, an attentive listener, and a genuinely wholesome person who exudes kindness, goodness, gentleness, humor, and humaneness. The world needs more physicians like yourself, who demonstrate profound respect and reverence for the mystery of illness.

I also want to express my gratefulness to Dr. Wasserman's staff, kindness and helpfulness abound in the medical office, especially Christina Cvijetinovic.

"All thinking that is imbued with wonder is graceful and gracious thinking."
John O'Donohue

Sincerely in the Risen Lord,

Fr. Tom Heron

Fr. Tom Heron

A more detailed letter of gratitude to a health professional after I was in his care. I am forever grateful for his compassion and bedside manner.

I have also written letters to doctors who have cared for me, thanking them for their compassion. Not all doctors are the same. I've sat in appointments where the doctor didn't even make eye contact, treating me like a file number. But I've also met doctors who took a genuine interest in my well-being. One doctor asked me what music I'd like to listen to as a distraction while administering a painful injection. It was a small gesture, but it made a difference. I wrote to him afterward, thanking him for the humanity he brought to his work. A letter like that can encourage someone to continue doing their job with kindness, to see their patients as people, not just cases.

Like a good doctor with a caring bedside manner for a patient, letter writing takes thought-provoked time, and that is one of its greatest strengths. If you're really trying to address an issue, clarify a misunderstanding, or convey a deeper meaning, you can't rush the process. A letter forces you to pause, to weigh your words carefully, and to ensure your intention comes across clearly. While it may not eliminate all misunderstandings, a well-crafted letter reduces confusion to its lowest common denominator. It opens the door for dialogue, allowing the recipient to ask questions or respond with their own perspective.

Letters can also confront issues with grace. They allow us to address differences or offer corrections without the heat of an argument clouding the exchange. "This is how I see it," you might write, "and perhaps your perspective is different." When you take the time to write such a letter, you invite engagement. Yes, you risk disagreement. Yes, you may face criticism or even opposition. But I would rather engage honestly—no matter the response—than live in isolation. A letter reveals more than what you think; it reveals that you care enough to try, to make an effort, and to invite others into a more meaningful exchange.

RISK AND RECIPROCITY

Jesus had a way of communicating that went beyond words. In Mark's Gospel, He reaches out to touch a leper, a radical act in His time, one that broke religious boundaries and societal norms.[6] To touch a leper meant becoming unclean, yet Jesus did it because He saw the human need beneath the stigma. He healed on the Sabbath, another act that defied the rules because

He refused to let religious formalities stand in the way of mercy.[7] When the woman suffering from hemorrhages for twelve years touched Him, He didn't recoil. He felt the power go out of Him and asked, *"Who touched me?"* He welcomed her act of faith.[8]

What does that have to do with letter writing? Everything. Like Jesus' actions, letters can cross boundaries. They can break through coldness, thoughtlessness, and isolation. A letter, written with care, can be a healing influence in someone's life. It can address a need, encourage a weary heart, or challenge a harmful perspective. It asks the writer to decide: Will you choose words that help or words that harm?

There's a certain emptiness we experience when kindness goes unacknowledged; a gift given with love that receives no response, or a heartfelt gesture met with silence. That emptiness is a reminder of how vital it is to respond, to acknowledge kindness, to reach back, and to choose healing over indifference.

Letter writing is not without risk. To write a letter is to put a piece of yourself into someone else's hands. Will they understand? Will they appreciate what you've tried to say? Or will they dismiss it altogether? These questions linger every time we write. And yet, the risk is worth taking because it is only by risking ourselves that we can build a bond of real human depth.

At its core, letter-writing yearns for reciprocity. You offer your humanity to someone else in the hope that the exchange will enrich both lives. In every letter I write, I ask myself: *Will this enrich the person receiving it? Will it inspire them, encourage them, or bring them hope?* And more often than not, the letters I receive in return do the same for me.

That is the beauty of the written word. It invites us to take a chance, to reach out, and to trust that what we offer will make a difference. Not every letter will receive a response. Some may be ignored, others misunderstood. But when the exchange works—when both writer and recipient are enriched—it confirms something essential: that we are not alone. That our humanity is meant to be shared.

The refrain remains constant: *Are you willing to risk giving your humanity to someone and, in turn, be enriched by their response?* It is the same risk Jesus took when He entered the lives of the broken, the outcast, and the lonely. He knew that not everyone would understand or accept Him. But He gave of Himself anyway, knowing that the gift of His presence could transform lives.

When you write a letter, you take part in that same sacred exchange. You give a piece of yourself, and in doing so, you invite someone else to do the same. It is an act of faith, hope, and love, and a small but meaningful way to affirm the best of the human condition.

Dear Father heron,
Tnauk you So much for
The Picture aud ice
cream treat
Love, Betty

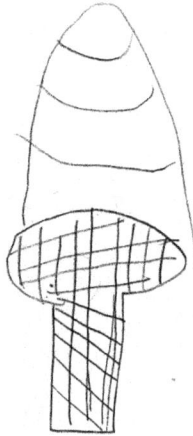

The innocence of a child, the maturity of a sage, the spirit of a saint.

If there is one thing I have learned, it is this: Life's most important lessons are often the simplest. Robert Fulghum wrote a great book called *All I Really Need to Know I Learned in Kindergarten*. How true! "Say please and thank you." "Be kind." "Share." These early lessons are the foundation of our relationships, and letter writing is one way we continue to live them out.

We live in a world that can be cold, hurried, and impersonal. But a letter—thoughtfully written—has the power to break through that icy hardness. It reminds us that we are not alone. It strengthens the bonds between us. It offers, in its own small way, a glimpse of the kingdom of God.

That outward motion to potentially touch the life of another is the more obvious mode of letter writing. However, in the next chapter, we'll explore a concept I discovered within myself when an important figure was on his way to Philadelphia some years ago.

And as we close, I challenge you to look within yourself: How can you offer yourself to another this week by way of a thoughtfully written letter?

EVERYONE THEN WHO LISTENS TO THESE WORDS OF MINE AND ACTS ON THEM WILL BE LIKE A WISE MAN WHO BUILT HIS HOUSE ON THE ROCK. (MATTHEW 7:24)

CHAPTER 2

The Grace of Transformation

HEALING THROUGH WRITING

Healing is as essential to the soul as air is to the lungs. In a world fraught with hurt, brokenness, and uncertainty, we carry unseen wounds: spiritual, emotional, and relational. For some, these wounds harden into resentment or despair, while for others, they become a doorway to grace. I've often reflected on the extraordinary gift of healing in my own life, not as a removal of suffering but as a transformation of it. Writing has been one of the most potent instruments of that transformation, a way to pour out what weighs heavily on the heart and invite God to shape it anew.

Writing demands a careful tempering of emotions. As a priest, I've learned that unfiltered words can wound more than they mend. Letters, in particular, have the power to build bridges, offering a space to express vulnerability and cultivate healing.

Healing through writing is not a new concept. St. Paul exemplifies it in his own letters, where he wrestles with his human frailty and divine calling. Paul's transformation from Saul, the persecutor of Christians, to Paul, the apostle of Christ, is a story of radical transformation through grace. Here was a man consumed by hatred, his life marked by the destruction of others. Yet, through an encounter with Christ, Saul was broken and remade. His past didn't vanish. It was redeemed, woven into his new identity as Paul, a tireless messenger of divine love. Writing, for Paul, became a vessel for proclaiming this truth, a means of uniting scattered faith communities and reminding them of the mystery of the Cross: that suffering, when embraced in faith, can lead to resurrection.

AN EXERCISE IN FAITH

March 11, 2014

1st Letter

COPY

His Holiness, Pope Francis
Apostolic Palace
00120 Vatican City

Dear Pope Francis,

Greetings from Conshohocken, Pennsylvania – St. Matthew's Parish.

Praised be to you Lord Jesus Christ!

As you complete your first year as Bishop of Rome, I want you to know that the parishioners of St. Matthew's rejoice in your warm, friendly, kind, compassionate, loving leadership style and service. You inspire all of us to follow your wonderful example in our relationships with one another.

Be assured of our daily prayers for you. Also, we hope to see you in Philadelphia in September 2015. May I be so bold and daring to invite you to St. Matthew's if your schedule permits. We are fourteen miles west of the mother church, the Cathedral Basilica of SS. Peter and Paul.

Know that the Mass you celebrated at Copacabana last year motivated us to profess our faith on Fayette Street as well. We are planning another outdoor Mass on Sunday, April 27, 2014 to celebrate Divine Mercy Sunday and the reception of First Holy Communion of 56 children.

I am most grateful to the rectory staff for their pastoral sensitivity and personal support: Mary Kay Sr. St. Herman, Val , Marie , Judy , Dave Drew , Bill and Sabrina

Ad multos annos!

"Our vocation is to restore divine order and proclaim the Good News." (Thomas Merton)

Listening, reading, praying Sacred Scripture, we are urged to pause and ponder: to give the words of Sacred Scripture their majestic due, our reverent, rejoicing attention.

Fraternally,

Tom

Fr. Tom Heron

Enclosure: photograph

My first letter to Pope Francis, March 11, 2014, inviting him to St. Matthew's during his upcoming visit to Philadelphia in 2015.

In March 2014, the ink flowed from my pen with enthusiasm, carrying the fresh and exciting idea of an invitation to Pope Francis to visit St. Matthew's Parish during his widely anticipated trip to Philadelphia for the World Meeting of Families in September 2015. My writing in that first letter was brimmed with optimism! It was Pope Francis's first year as Bishop of Rome, and his example of humility and love had captured the hearts of so many, including myself. But this was no mere logistical request. It was an act of hope and connection, a desire to draw a bridge between a parish community in Conshohocken and the man who has inspired millions in short order.

The letter was equal parts admiration and invitation, a reflection of both my hope and naivety. I described our parish as a vibrant community longing to welcome him. I spoke of our outdoor Masses, the joys of our parishioners, and even mentioned the "Dorothy Day Hospitality Suite" we had prepared for his stay. It was a bold ask but one made in faith. In retrospect, however, this moment marked the beginning of a spiritual exercise that would span multiple years.

The letters soon became more than an invitation, but a way of processing the complex realities of parish life and personal grief. In writing to Pope Francis, I found a sense of purpose and solace. It was a therapy of the spirit. These letters became both a reflection of my inner struggles and an offering of hope to another who surely carried the weight of the world's suffering on his shoulders.

There is an alchemy in the act of writing. What begins as a swirl of emotions takes shape in words and, through reflection, becomes something deeper. Writing requires that we move beyond our initial impulses, tempering raw feelings so that what emerges is not only cathartic but constructive. It's a skill I've honed over the years, learning that unchecked emotions can do more harm than good, even when they are honestly expressed.

The letters I wrote to Pope Francis unfolded against a backdrop of significant change and upheaval in my parish. St. Matthew's was merging with three other churches, a decision born of necessity but fraught with tension. By 2014, the Catholic Church in Conshohocken faced declining numbers, aging congregations, and financial strain. The mergers were a painful process, involving the closure of beloved churches like St. Gertrude's and SS. Cosmas and Damian. It was a time of difficult pastoral decisions, and as I navigated these challenges, I turned to the act of writing to process and attempt to find peace and meaning.

July 14, 2014

His Holiness, Pope Francis
Apostolic Palace
00120 Vatican City

2nd letter

Dear Pope Francis,

Greetings again from Conshohocken, Pennsylvania – the newly merged St. Matthew's Parish that now includes St. Gertrude, St. Mary, and SS Cosmas & Damian.

Yesterday, I was installed by Bishop Dan Thomas as the new pastor of four merged churches in Conshohocken and West Conshohocken and you think you have weighty matters of state to address.

I continue to pray that you will be able to visit in September 22-27, 2015 for the World Meeting of Families and possibly come to Conshohocken which is fourteen miles west of the Cathedral Basilica of SS. Peter and Paul.

I am enclosing a copy of the St. Vincent de Paul Society report.

Finally, I ask that you pray for a faithful priest friend – Msgr. Dan Murray who died on June 26, 2014. Dan was my spiritual director for forty-four years. He is a great loss to me. May he rest in peace eternally.

Friends remain our touchstones, fellow travelers even after death. They are both missing and present to us at all times—the paradox of felt absence and real presence.

Fraternally,

Tom

Fr. Tom Heron

Enclosure

My second letter to Pope Francis, July 14, 2014, sharing updates and asking for prayers.

The second letter to Pope Francis, sent in July 2014, reflects the dual burdens of grief and hope. That summer, I lost my dear friend and spiritual director, Monsignor Dan Murray. For 44 years, Dan had been my confidant, offering wisdom and support through every chapter of my priesthood. In the letter, I shared my prayers for unity and healing in our community, echoing Pope Francis's own ministry of reconciliation.

August 20, 2014

His Holiness, Pope Francis
Apostolic Palace
00120 Vatican City

4th letter

Dear Pope Francis,

My prayers are with you as you grieve the physical loss of your niece Valeria and her children Antonio and Jose.

May your faith in the Risen Lord be a source of strength and comfort to you and your family in the days ahead.

Weeping is the eloquence of sorrow. It is an unstammering orator, needing no interpreter, but understood by all. Tears are to be understood even when words fail! We need to learn that tears are liquid prayers of intercession which will wear its way right into the very heart of mercy, despite the stony difficulties which obstruct the way.

Be assured of my prayers that your nephew Emanuel will recover from this tragic highway crash in Argentina—God willing.

Tolstoy wrote, **"Whatever answers any kind of faith ever gives to anyone, every one of these answers gives an infinite meaning to the finite life of man, a meaning that is not destroyed by suffering, privation, and death."**

Fraternally,

Tom

Fr. Tom Heron

This time, offering prayers for the Pope, as he mourned losses of his own.

By September 2014, my letters began to reflect a deeper longing, as well as my understanding of the Pope's humanity. I wrote about the tragic loss of his niece and her two children, offering my prayers and a reflection on how faith helps us navigate grief. This was not a letter of invitation; it was a letter of solidarity and prayer. I sought to offer the Pope the same consolation I had received in moments of loss: the assurance that death is never the final word and that the communion of saints binds us together in hope. Through my words, I sought to extend a bridge to the Pope himself, who, though a global leader, remains a man in need of comfort like any of us.

SHARING HUMANITY

His Holiness, Pope Francis
Apostolic Palace
00120 Vatican City

November 20, 2014

Dear Pope Francis,

Greetings from Conshohocken! The whole country eagerly awaits your visit to the U.S.A. and to the city of Philadelphia.

My dad's death and Dan's death, both, have had a profound impact in my life. I am still trying to sort it all out.

I write to you for two reasons, one, today is the 11th Anniversary of my Mom's death and two I had a vivid dream of Dan early this morning.

When Dan was in the hospitals, Lankenau and Abington Lansdale, Abramson Nursing Care and St. Joseph's Manor he yearned to have a connection with the outside world, especially to the changes of the seasons. He mused frequently about being cut off from all that he loved and cherished. "It seems that I am becoming more disconnected."

I would ask Dan what can I do to help him be reconnected. After a ponderous pause, Dan would say "not much".

"Tom, please do not abandon me. Make sure you come and visit me once and a while at SS Peter and Paul".

"Tom, I need you to keep vigil with me—praying, meditating, or simply talking with me, to help relieve my anxiety, fears, and loneliness."

Dan's death of 5 months ago and my Dad's death of 57 years ago, call me today to be more generous in prayer and more fearless in ministry. Their deaths are painful, but also full of grace.

"Every problem has two handles.
You can grab it by the handle of fear or
the handle of hope." (Margaret Mitchell)

Winston Churchill once said, "It is a good thing to collect quotes. The qualities, when engraved upon the memory, give you good thoughts." Quotes are meant to be carried with you. They help you see things differently.

Dan Murray had the uncanny ability to draw out a smile from within my soul.

The teaching of the Communion of Saints consoles me.

The abundant Grace of the announcement of your coming to Philadelphia had a wonderful impact on the whole Archdiocese of Philadelphia.

Warmly with inner Light of the Holy Spirit,

Fr. Tom Heron

Here, I confide in Pope Francis, as I was experiencing sorrow in all of my losses through the years.

As 2014 came to a close, the childlike wonder akin to a young believer writing to Old Saint Nick had transformed into the familiarity and fondness of writing to an old friend.

This time of year was particularly reflective of a season of deeply felt loss in my life. Dan Murray's recent death was still fresh in my heart, his absence a gaping void in my weekly rhythm of spiritual counsel and friendship. Dan was the rock on which I leaned as a priest, and in the last two years of his life, our roles had reversed. I became the one offering care, sitting with him as he gently drifted away from the sharpness of intellect to the simplicity of spoken nursery rhymes.

Yet, it wasn't only Dan's passing that weighed on me as I wrote. The losses of my parents lingered too; my mother eleven years earlier and my father before I was even five years old. Though years had passed since their deaths, the grief had not entirely subsided. I was reminded that grief has its own timeline. Loss becomes part of the fabric of our lives, woven through relationships and memories. Time does not erase it but transforms it, and in this transformation lies the paradox I reflected upon in that letter: the felt absence of our loved ones and their real presence that we can still experience through faith, memory, and love.

The communion of saints, one of the most consoling teachings of the Catholic Church, holds that those who have gone before us remain connected to us in ways that transcend the limits of time and space. They are not lost to us but await us in the place prepared for them, in the fullness of God's love. That belief sustained me as I wrote to Pope Francis, pouring out my thoughts on the interconnectedness of past, present, and future.

I shared with him my anticipation of his visit to Philadelphia the following September, nearly ten months away. In a way, his impending arrival mirrored that hope of reconnection, a promise of presence to heal a sense of disconnection. His coming, I wrote, could help heal the collective wounds of our parish, just as I hoped it might touch the deep grief in my own heart. It was not merely his physical arrival that I longed for but the healing, the renewal of spirit that such an encounter could bring.

This seventh letter was, in many ways, a meditation on loss and hope, a reflection on how the journey of faith carries us through sorrow into the light of God's enduring presence. It expressed a yearning not just for the Pope's physical presence but for the deeper reassurance of the Church's connection, a reminder that even in absence, there is the promise of eternal communion. In those moments of writing, I found a measure of peace, a glimmer of the healing I prayed for so fervently.

HUMOR HEALS, TOO

Amid the challenges, there were moments of grace and humor that found their way into the letters. Expanding upon our shared humanity as brothers in the clergy, I wanted humor to shine through in my letters to Pope Francis.

In March 2015, as Holy Week approached, I wrote about the modest, earthly symbols we use to celebrate this sacred time: palm branches, bread, wine, fire, and water. "How frail!" I reflected. Yet, in their frailty, these signs hold the power to express the yearning of our hearts. The same could be said of my letters. Though simple, they carried the weight of a parish's hopes and the vulnerability of a priest seeking to serve God faithfully.

As the letters continued, they became interwoven with stories from parish life ... moments that revealed the presence of God in unexpected places. In one letter, I shared the story of our

Pentecost dove release, an annual tradition that always brought a smile. A young boy, watching the dove take flight, turned to his sister and said, "It's a dove, not a pigeon!" That simple remark became a metaphor for the sacraments: outward signs that point us to deeper spiritual realities.

Another letter introduced a faith-filled household whose children asked the most delightful theological questions. One Sunday, after hearing my homily on God's playful presence, a young boy asked, "Will Father release a falcon next week?" These moments of childlike wonder reminded me why I became a priest in the first place: to nurture faith, especially in its most innocent and sincere forms.

And then, there was Sister St. Herman. A wise and playful presence in our rectory, she often had a way of lightening even the heaviest moments. At one point, when the intensity of the Pope's visit to Philadelphia reached its peak, she quipped, "Well, Tom, if the Pope doesn't show up, at least I can put on a white cassock and make an appearance!" It was a line delivered with her signature mix of humor and affection, a reminder not to take ourselves too seriously.

As 2015 progressed, it became crystal clear that Pope Francis would not visit St. Matthew's. The logistics were impossible. The Schuylkill Expressway was closed, and the Pope's itinerary focused on the prison, the seminary, and other prominent venues. I understood the necessity, but it felt like a missed opportunity. A parish is the heart of the Church, and his presence at a parish would have been a great gift to the entire Archdiocese.

Still, I continued writing. The letters became less about persuading the Pope to visit and more about sharing reflections, hopes, and prayers. In one letter, I included a list of ways to nurture a hopeful heart, inspired by his own writings on faith and joy. It was a way of giving back to someone whose ministry had given so much to me. In another, I fondly reflected upon my grandfather's wisdom and influence.

March 11, 2015

His Holiness, Pope Francis
Apostolic Palace
00120 Vatican City

Dear Pope Francis,

The favorite daily miracle of Jesus is His merciful, forgiving love.

As we approach the Feast of St. Patrick next week, I recall with fondness my grandfather—John Heron. He was born in Draperstown, Ireland. He celebrated his birthday twice a year March 17th and December 25th. He was a most joyful man who loved the simple delights of life—his hands in the earth—gardener, a shared meal and storytelling.

My grandfather was a wonderful storyteller. The common theme of everyone of his stories—he was the hero.

His formal education ended in the fourth grade. I am enclosing two poems he gave me—one when I was 11 years old and one a month before my ordination. Enjoy!

Reverence is an unskippable virtue in any renewal in the Church.

Reverence is the virtue that combines wonder, gratitude and humility.

"The Catholic Church glories in all Christ's actions, but her greatest glory is the cross." *(St. Cyril of Jerusalem)*

'If we walk without the Cross…then we are not our Lord's disciples. We are worldly people. We may be bishops, priests, cardinals, popes. But we are not disciples of the Lord'. *(Pope Francis)*

Fraternally,

Fr. Tom Heron

One year after my first letter to Pope Francis, I write again, sharing my Irish heritage and admiration for my grandfather.

SUFFERING AND GRACE

A decade later, as I reflect on these letters in earnest, I see them as a mirror of St. Paul's writings. Paul's confessional tone—his acknowledgment of weakness and his reliance on grace—resonates deeply with my own journey. In his letter to the Romans, Paul writes, "For I do not do the good I want, but the evil I do not want is what I do" (Romans 7:19). This tension between human frailty and divine strength is one I know well. It is a reminder that healing is not about erasing our struggles but allowing God to transform them.

Even though Romans is right after the Acts of the Apostles, scholars believe it's probably one of the last letters that he wrote, and it's his longest letter by far. He's trying to bring together all these loose elements into some unified pattern for the benefit of everybody who claims to be a disciple of Jesus. It's a terrific work. It is, without a doubt, his best work.

He's saying that living the Gospel is always an ongoing challenge. It's not something that you can ascent to once and think you're done with it. The Gospel will challenge you to love your enemies, just as Jesus calls. The Gospel will always challenge you to a higher or better way of living. You must have the virtue of humility to be able to accommodate its call.

There's healing in the process. Paul himself, in his letter to the Colossians, described rejoicing in his sufferings and finding joy in offering them for the sake of the Church.[9] Writing to Pope Francis allowed me to echo that sentiment, finding solace even in the absence of a reply. The act of writing became my answer.

THE TRUE MEANING OF MY WORK

July 19, 2016

His Holiness, Pope Francis
Apostolic Palace
00120 Vatican City

Dear Pope Francis,

I am writing to inform you of two new ministries that came to me during my daily swim recently.

The first ministry is writing letters to two year olds. This simple, personal touch has been fruitful to the Charlotte's and Sean's of the parish and their parents and siblings. I have included a few sample copies and a few photos.

The second ministry involves handing out small wooden crosses (given to me by Sister St. Herman) to the folks in the pew while I deliver my homily. On the weekend when the Good Samaritan is proclaimed (Luke 10:25-37) I ask each person to pray for someone they know who is down on their luck and in a ditch. The week Jesus visited His good friends Martha & Mary (Luke 10:38-42). I ask parishioners to pray for people who suffer from worry and anxiety.

I hope you are well. Pray for us in the U.S.A. as we prepare to elect a new president—Donald Trump or Hillary Clinton. Mr. Trump represents a huge risk. However, honesty requires that this risk be weighted against a clear-eyed look at the certainties Mrs. Clinton would bring to the White House—21st century American liberalism that no longer pretends to achieve results for the common good. Prayers please!

Nothing great is ever achieved without enthusiasm.

It is one of the most beautiful compensations of life that no man can sincerely try to help another without helping himself.

If you laugh, you think, and you cry, that's a full day. That's a heck of a day. You do that seven days a week, you're going to have something special.

Events have a meaning beyond what can be immediately known.

Gratefully,

Fr. Tom Heron

While the Pope never visited St. Matthew's during his trip to Philedelphia, I still "kept in touch."

The final letter I wrote to Pope Francis in July 2016 was not an invitation or a request. It was a reflection, an update, and a farewell of sorts. By then, I had come to see the letters not as a means to an end but as an end in themselves. They were a way of entering into dialogue with God, of seeking healing and offering it in turn. They were, no question, a means of therapy.

They helped me work through things I was going through at the time that I absolutely needed to work through.

And once the letters stopped, I miraculously received a piece of mail. Rushing to open it and read the ultimate wisdom of its contents, my heart was filled with uproarious joy as the words jumped off the page. Thank you, Sister St. Herman, for the much-needed chuckle!

My Dear Tom,

Thank the Lord that someone just told me that you were away on vacation. I was very concerned about you when the letters stopped coming in!

Welcome back!

Your BFF,

Pope Francis

Sister St. Herman's humor in all its glory!

The world is fraught with a lot of hurt, and if you consciously live in this world, you're going to experience that hurt firsthand or, at minimum, secondhand. The person of Jesus comes to refresh, heal, forgive, uplift, and put you on a new path of grace. That's what happens in the sacrament of reconciliation, but it can also happen with any contact with any person. As a priest, you meet people who are overwhelmed by hurt. You are to listen and try to bring healing to their difficult circumstances. One way to heal that I urge my fellow students of Christ to engage in is, of course, writing.

So, as persistent as I was in my writing to Pope Francis, I will remain persistent with you, my readers, in my invitation: Write. Write to someone you admire, someone you love, or even someone who has caused you pain. Write to God. Pour out your heart on paper, and let the act of writing become a space of grace and healing. You may find, as I did, that the words you write have the power to transform, not only the one who receives them but the one who writes them.

As Oscar Hammerstein said, "...a writer gives himself away if he is writing honestly."[10] All writers reveal their obsessions and preoccupations, and half the time, they are not even conscious of it. In the next chapter, we explore how we can make productive use of our time in musing over those obsessions and preoccupations as we enter the realm of letters of opinion.

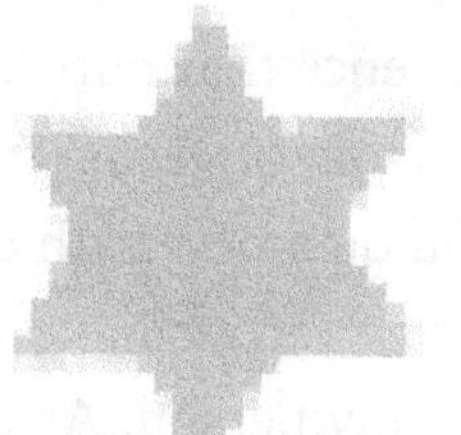

It is with great pleasure that I accept your million invitations to visit Saint Matthew Parish. My acceptance came from a variety of reasons----

---- My presence will at least stop the US Postal Service making daily visits to the Vatican

----since you stormed heaven I have little choice.

----I understand you have no kitchen accommodations so I will not stay for any meals-however "gluten free" meals are not my choice.

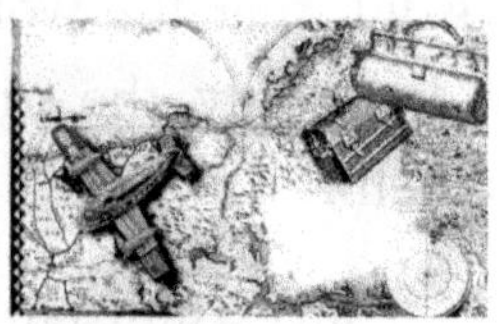

----To relieve some parking pressures I will arrive by helicopter- can I use the school roof?

---- my arrival will be about 8 AM so I will not interfere with your swimming session.

Thank you again for your warm hospitality. My gift to you will be three weeks at the Vatican. This will give your staff a little time to recupe.

Happy Christmas, Francis

Greetings from the Vatican

Some of Sister St. Herman's best work!

CHAPTER 3

The Risk and Reward of Authenticity

LETTERS OF OPINION

In the life of a priest, words hold immense weight. Words spoken from the pulpit may reach a congregation, but words written to be broadcast into the public arena can resonate far beyond church walls. Writing letters of opinion, for me, has always been an act of faith and courage and a means of amplifying the Gospel message in a world that often resists its truth. These letters are not just a reflection of my beliefs; they are an invitation to dialogue, an effort to bring light to complex issues, and, at times, a bold declaration of conviction. Lately, I have sensed an attempt to silence, ignore, or dismiss a faith viewpoint from the public "square."

The act of writing a letter of opinion is an audacious one. To send one's thoughts out into the open is to expose the heart to both affirmation and rejection. Writing these letters is not merely a habit but a vocation. The pulpit, after all, was never meant to be confined to wood and stone. It is meant to reverberate across boundaries, reaching the ears of those in need of encouragement, correction, or simply a reminder of shared humanity.

The first letter I ever wrote for publication emerged from my time in the seminary. It was a reflection on Mark's Gospel, particularly on the call to take up one's cross and follow Christ. John Foley, the editor of *The Catholic Standard and Times,* taught me a lot about writing. Even when my opinion contradicted popular sentiments, he gave it space in print. I learned early on that writing a letter of opinion doesn't mean you'll change everyone's mind. It's about being faithful to the truth as you see it.

When I sit down to write a letter of opinion, I feel the weight of responsibility, not just as a priest but as a citizen of the world. There's risk involved, of course. You're opening yourself up to criticism, to misunderstanding, and even to rejection. Yet, as Christians, are we not called to risk for the sake of truth? St. Paul reminds us in his letter to Timothy: "...proclaim the word; be persistent whether it is convenient or inconvenient; convince, reprimand, encourage through all patience and teaching" (2 Timothy 4:2). Writing letters of opinion is my way of living that call.

Over the years, I've penned letters addressing everything from societal violence to the failings of public figures, each one a testament to my belief in the transformative power of words. Yet, I knew that words alone were insufficient. They had to be grounded in love, tempered by humility, and aimed at building bridges, not walls.

A CALL FOR REVERENCE: THE NFL AND DOMESTIC VIOLENCE

September 19, 2014

Philadelphia Inquirer
Opinion/Editorials

Much ink has been spilled lately over domestic violence, especially among NFL players, Ray Rice, Greg Hardy, Adrian Peterson, and Ray McDonald to name a few.

What about verbal violence? When verbal violence has become so prevalent in our society, so accepted, so casual that rudeness, crudeness, and blasphemy are the everyday norm, does it surprise anyone that physical violence is on the rise and not just among NFL players?

In my judgment, there is a definite connection between verbal violence and physical domestic violence. We need to recover a reverence for words, a reverence for life, a reverence for creation to transform the disorder of violence into the order of harmony.

Father Tom Heron

This letter to the editor was my attempt to step back and reflect: how do we prevent such heinous acts of violence? Perhaps it begins with something small but essential, checking the impulse to speak with hostility.

One letter that stands out to me was written in 2014 in response to a series of domestic violence scandals involving NFL players like Ray Rice and Greg Hardy. The media's coverage of these cases was exhaustive, yet it seemed to miss a deeper point. Violence of any kind, left unchecked, will spread to other things. In my letter, I argued that violence does not begin with a physical act. It begins with words. Verbal violence —so casual and pervasive in our society—lays the foundation for the physical violence that follows.

What I'm trying to say is that we need to recover our reverence for words in order to recover our reverence for life and our reverence for creation in order to transform the disorder of violence into a human order of harmony and peace. If there is a recurrent pattern of physical violence, for example, how do we correct it and redirect it?

One strategy I employed to spread my words was to send a similar letter to the local paper because I realized that a whole lot of people in Conshohocken did not read *The Philadelphia Inquirer*, which kind of surprised me at first. Collingdale, where I grew up, was a similar town to Conshohocken—almost 10,000 people—and almost everyone read the *Inquirer*. I delivered that paper and *The Evening Bulletin*.

The letter sparked some debate, but that's what I hoped for. Writing letters of opinion is not about pleasing everyone. It's about planting seeds of thought, even if they take time to grow.

A TIME FOR HEALING: GEORGE FLOYD AND NATIONAL GRIEF

Letter to the Editor:

A former teacher of mine would repeat this phrase often in class, "We correct old evils with a passion that mars the new good." What this country and the world has witnessed this past week confirms the truth of that statement. George Floyd's death was raw evil. Racism, violence, rioting, looting are all old evils. Peaceful protest is necessary and is the best method for correcting these ugly evils.

What we have seen is wrongheaded leadership that allowed destructive anger and foolishness to rule the streets of our cities due to the lack of fortitude and fairness in our leaders. Everyone suffers by this mayhem, especially the poor and minority neighborhoods. Businesses endure property damage and now absorb new costs.

Ernest Hemingway offers sage advice during this chaotic time, "The world breaks everyone, and afterward many are strong in the broken places." Some of the noblest human traits flourish in the soil of suffering. Compassion and kindness, fortitude and patience, sympathy and humility-these are part of the rich harvest that can ripen from the dark seeds of pain. Whether or not we become strong in the broken places depends ultimately on our attitude toward suffering. If we realize that suffering is our common lot and that it can help us grow in spirit and grace, then we can indeed use it to grow in the broken places.

Father Tom Heron
St. Matthews
Conshohocken, PA

This letter was written in the wake of George Floyd's death, a moment that shook the world's conscience. I wanted to offer more than outrage. I wanted to reflect. If we hope to break cycles of violence, we must begin by tending to the soil of our own hearts. Words matter. Compassion matters. And suffering, if embraced with grace, can become the ground where holiness grows.

The murder of George Floyd in 2020 was a watershed moment for our country. The pain and anger it unleashed were palpable, and rightly so. Yet, as I reflected on this tragedy, I found myself asking: How do we channel this collective grief into something constructive? How do we confront the evil of racism without letting it harden our hearts?

In my letter following Floyd's death, I used the power of a quote, which is something common in my letter writing. I quoted Ernest Hemingway in this entry: "The world breaks everyone, and afterward, many are strong in the broken places."[11]

Everyone has to be on guard that evil at this national level can get even more evil if we're not vigilant or attentive to its source. How can we tap into virtues like compassion, kindness, fortitude, peace, sympathy, and humility in the face of this brokenness?

You often hear of a store getting robbed, and people anonymously and out of the blue write a check to the corner store owner so he doesn't have to worry about it. I got robbed when I was serving at Good Shepherd. They might've gotten $2,500 dollars, but they did significant damage. *The Inquirer* covered that story, and I received a check for $10,000 from a Jewish couple from New Jersey.

And, in the spirit of the topic of this book, I did only what I knew… I wrote a letter of gratitude and visited them. I received more money from outside sources than I needed to cover all of the costs of damages. So, I used the surplus to give back to the community. That's the power of writing: the word is spread, the community is informed, and they typically appear in droves. And as a result, it all returns to the community at large!

This letter was not about offering solutions. It was about inviting readers to reflect on their own role in healing a broken world. Writing it was not easy. The temptation to preach is always there, especially for a priest. But I knew that this was a moment to listen as much as to speak; to stand with others in their grief, not above them.

I put my pants on the same way everybody else does. I have to learn and grow from what's going on in the world, too. I'm not above anyone. I'm with you in being challenged by these tragedies.

THE COURAGE TO CRITIQUE: HILLARY CLINTON AND THE 'DEPLORABLES'

Letter to the Editor:

I disagree with E.J. Dionne 's assessment of Hillary Clinton being authentically religious and a woman of faith. Mrs. Clinton says she "tries to tell the truth" when she speaks, except for when it is personally or politically inconvenient. Truth telling is a fundamental and indisputable tenet of faith and religion.

Where is the social justice in her long-standing pattern of cronyism? Too often her friends benefit and the less fortunate get forgotten. Her obligation to the poor, in my judgment, is just lip service.

The only time I can recall Mrs. Clinton getting her hands dirty was when she cleaned out the White House of furniture and other artifacts that she claimed as her own.

I have yet to see beyond her arrogance and elitism. For example, her recent put-down of Trump supporters as "deplorables".

Mrs. Clinton, because she is a public figure, has demonstrated repeatedly in the public square that she is morally and ethically challenged.

No one is exempt of **"weeds and wheat"** in his or her life. Humility is taking ownership of both the strengths and weaknesses of our character and personality.

Fr. Tom Heron

A public letter on the moral weight of leadership and the call for truth in both word and witness.

During the 2016 presidential campaign, I wrote a letter responding to Hillary Clinton's infamous "basket of deplorables" comment. I found her words troubling, not just because they were divisive but because they overlooked a fundamental truth: We are all a mix of weeds and wheat. None of us is wholly good or wholly bad. Humility demands that we acknowledge this about ourselves and about others.

> LET THE ONE AMONG YOU WHO IS WITHOUT SIN BE THE FIRST TO THROW A STONE. (JOHN 8:7)

This letter stirred quite a response: about a dozen letters back to me! Two of them were favorable, the rest humbling. Some accused me of endorsing Donald Trump, which was not my intention. My goal was simply to remind readers that humility is the foundation of any meaningful dialogue. It's fascinating how people will read what they want to see rather than what's actually written. But that's part of the dialogue, isn't it? Letters like that remind me to clarify, deepen my arguments, and approach the next letter with even greater care.

Dear Rev. Heron,

I agree with E.J. Dionne's assessment of Hillary Clinton as opposed to you in your letter today's Inquirer. Your attempt to put her down obviously encourages your parishioners and other Catholics to vote for Trump-an ignorant, racist bully who publicly makes fun of people with disabilities. **As opposed to Pope Francis,** Trump is a man who claims climate change is a hoax and would condemn us and our grandchildren to futures of floods, fires and climate refugees beyond anything we have yet seen. **Do you truly believe there is equivalency between anything Clinton has said or done and Trump's public condemnation of entire groups of people- Mexicans, immigrants and Muslims?** Trump has the temperament and attention span of a very challenged 14 year old. As president he would lack any patience or ability to hear differing views and make reasoned decisions. His hand on top of the military or nuclear weapons should scare you far more than any actions or statements from Clinton, a flawed but far more informed and social justice oriented candidate than Donald Trump. When has he ever shown any humility and come close to taking ownership of the strengths and weaknesses of his character and personality?

This anonymous response to my letter reflects the deep political and moral tensions of the time. While I've omitted the writer's name to protect their privacy, their words reveal the passion and concern shared by many on all sides of public discourse.

And that's the nature of writing a letter of opinion. You're not aiming for unanimous applause. You're aiming to provoke thought. The blowback represents the risk inherent in writing letters of opinion. You can't control how your words will be received. But as a priest, I believe it's a risk worth taking. The Gospel itself is risky. It calls us to love our enemies, to forgive those who wrong us, and to speak the truth even when it's unpopular. If we shy away from those challenges, we betray the very message we're called to live.

Sadly, of the many responses I received, plenty of them took liberties to attack the Catholic church, which I, of course, represent. As a priest, I need to balance my personal opinion, which might differ from the common perception of the church's teaching. There are issues that my personal opinion might not be in harmony with regarding the church's teaching, but it's more the case that people's perception of the church's teaching is not always rooted in absolute truth. Every person is entitled to his or her opinion. I just hope it's an informed opinion and based on the facts. To this day, you still meet people who do not have a developed understanding of why the church teaches on certain issues in the ways that it does. They don't have the reasoning and the logic that enables them. A lot of times, the church gets perceived as a superior or definitive word. "End of conversation," people think. I don't think that is the church's way. The church takes a position but should be in very active dialogue to tweak its position along with the times. We as human beings and Christ followers have to understand how the church got to this position and what variables that weren't present years ago are now present to make a change in that position. Not understanding those simple truths is what leaves churchgoers stuck in their ways and not progressing forward and walking with Jesus.

A VOICE FOR THE VOICELESS: LETTERS TO PRESIDENT BIDEN

Dear President Biden,

The prophet Isaiah says, Woe to "those who call evil good, and good evil" (Is. 5:20). Abortion is the direct killing of an innocent, defenseless, voiceless baby. Abortion is raw evil. Call things by their true names, no matter how politically incorrect it may be. We need to get back to simple first things: the goodness of goodness and the evilness of evilness.

You are a prodigal Roman Catholic who has lost his way by calling abortion reproductive health care service. Something as simple as the deliberate murder of babies in the womb is clearly self-deception on your part. St. Paul's encouragement to you is: "Awake, O sleeper, rise up from the dead, and Christ will give you his light"(Eph. 5:14).

Truth incarnate is right here in front of you and in front of me, just as truly as Jesus was right there in front of the Pharisees and in front of Pilate, waiting for us to come to the Risen Lord with open minds and open heart so that the Risen Lord can dwell in our souls.

Our mission in life is to live the truth. The grace-filled season of Lent is about sacrifice. What do we have to sacrifice if we are to know and live the truth? Our pride? Our self-deception?

Be assured of my prayers for you, Jill and family during the remaining days of Lent. I will also fast and give alm for your intentions . No lie.

In Corde Christi,

Fr. Tom Heron

P.S. Mr. Biden, the Constitution guarantees the right to life, liberty, and the pursuit of happiness. Overturning Roe v. Wade the Supreme Court has NOT taken away any Constitutional rights. I could not help but notice Vice-President Kamala Harris deleted life in her remarks quoting the Constitution. That is sad. Very sad.

A Lenten letter to President Biden, written in truth and charity, urging clarity on life, faith, and moral leadership.

My letters to President Joe Biden are among the most personal I've ever written. As a Catholic, I felt compelled to challenge him on the polarizing issue of abortion, which I believe is a grave injustice against the most vulnerable among us.

As recently as 2006, then-Senator Biden stated that "abortion is not a choice or a right; it's always a tragedy." He spoke then with a clarity that resonated with Catholic teaching: that abortion harms not just the child who is killed but also the mother, who carries an indelible wound from such an act. The memory of it may be numbed for a time, but it never truly disappears.

Somewhere along the way, though, Biden's words and policies shifted to align with a worldview that trivializes human life. Gone are the days when the Democratic Party platform spoke of abortion as something that should be "safe, legal, and rare." Now, it seems, science and humanity are cast aside. We know that a fetus develops all its organs by twelve weeks, can feel pain around twenty-five weeks, and could survive outside the womb after the twenty-third week.[12] Yet, abortion policies have been proposed to ignore these truths, even suggesting acts so extreme that babies who survive abortion attempts are denied medical care. This is not healthcare. It's cruelty, plain and simple. And to remain silent about such an atrocity is to be complicit in its perpetuation.

I cannot remain silent.

August 21, 2022

President Joe Biden
The White House
1600 Pennsylvania Ave. N.W.
Washington, DC 20500

Dear President Biden,

You have been duped and you let yourself be duped on the issue of abortion.

Abortion is a violent, barbaric, cruel action. Abortion is child murder. Period.

Abortion is America's greatest horror story. To butcher an innocent, defenseless, voiceless baby in the name of choice, in the name of health care, in the name of privacy is to be sold a bill of lies. Abortion is always a tragedy as you once believed.

I pray that you have the courage you once had and change your mind and heart on this moral evil of abortion. It is medical malpractice and social dehumanization. There is a name, a face, and an untold story for every unborn child destroyed by abortion.

Fr. Tom Heron

Fr. Tom Heron

P.S. Stop being so vindictive and spiteful to your so-called enemies.

This letter was written as a plea to President Biden's conscience … a call to reclaim moral clarity on the dignity of unborn life.

Abortion is an act of violence, not only against the child but also against the social fabric of humanity. When we normalize violence at this most vulnerable stage of life, we pave the way for a broader acceptance of violence in all its forms. I wrote to Biden about this in a letter that began with a stark accusation: "You have been duped." It's a phrase borrowed from the prophet Jeremiah: "You duped me, Lord, and I let myself be duped." (Jeremiah 20:7). I used it to challenge Biden's moral blind spots; his willingness to embrace the rhetoric of reproductive rights while ignoring the humanity of the unborn child.

These letters were not written in anger but in sorrow. They were marked by both urgency and respect. I saw in Biden, a man who had once spoken passionately about the tragedy of abortion, only to later embrace policies that ignored its human cost. My goal was not to attack him but to call him back to the principles of his faith ... to remind him that freedom for the mother cannot come at the expense of the baby's life.

THE WHITE HOUSE

WASHINGTON

February 24, 2023

Father Tom Heron
Norristown, Pennsylvania

Dear Father Heron,

Thank you for writing to me. In overturning *Roe v. Wade*, the Supreme Court has taken away a constitutional right from the American people to make the most intimate decisions about their health care and families without government interference. Now, fundamental rights to privacy, autonomy, freedom, and equality have been denied to millions of women across the country, with grave implications for their health, lives, and well-being.

What we're witnessing is a giant step backward in much of our country, but let me be clear: Access to reproductive care is health care. Vice President Harris and I will fight for the freedom of all people to build their own future and determine their own destiny.

That's why I signed an Executive Order that safeguards access to reproductive health care services such as medication abortion and contraception and ensures emergency medical care. It also protects the privacy of patients and their access to accurate information and promotes the safety and security of everyone who seeks and provides health care services. Finally, this Executive Order makes sure that the entire Federal Government is coordinated in our efforts to protect reproductive rights and access to health care across America.

The Supreme Court and its allies are committed to moving America backward with fewer rights, less autonomy, and politicians invading the most personal of decisions. This decision affects everyone, and the American people must continue to demand that Congress enshrine the protections of *Roe v. Wade* into federal law. I believe Congress should do so with a simple majority vote, but if Congress lacks the votes to do that now, you need to make your voices heard. Our daughters and granddaughters deserve the same rights as their mothers and grandmothers.

This fight is not over. To find out more about your right to access reproductive health care, visit ReproductiveRights.gov.

Sincerely,

This official reply from President Biden reveals the deep divide on life and liberty in our nation. Though we differ on what constitutes justice for the unborn, I share it here as a record of correspondence and conviction. **Note:** *Quick research revealed this exact letter has been sent to other citizens concerned with President Biden's stance on abortion.*

When Biden responded to my letter on Feb. 24, 2023, his words were predictable. He wrote about the freedom of women to make "intimate decisions about their health care and families without government interference." But what about the freedom of the unborn child? Who speaks for the baby, the one who is voiceless, defenseless, and innocent? Biden's response completely ignored this fundamental question. He argued that "reproductive care is health care," yet failed to address how this applies to the baby, whose very existence is denied in this equation.

The Church teaches that there are rare and tragic circumstances, such as ectopic pregnancies, where medical intervention results in the unintended death of a baby to save the mother's life.[13] This is guided by the principle of double effect, addressing a grave medical condition while recognizing the tragic consequence. But these instances are not the norm. What we see today is a culture where abortion is a first resort rather than a last. As of 2023, sixty-three percent of abortions now occur through medication and are partially administered at home.[14] The "choice" Biden championed has become a solitary act, detached from the sacredness of life and the communal responsibility to nurture and protect it.

The response I received from the White House—a defense of reproductive rights—was disappointing but not surprising. Still, I believe these letters mattered. Writing them was an act of faith, a way of bearing witness to the sanctity of life in a culture that so often denies it.

September 27, 2022

President Joe Biden
The White House
1600 Pennsylvania Ave. N.W.
Washington, DC 20500

Dear President Biden,

In 1933 George Bernard Shaw visited the United States and remarked, "You Americans are so fearful of dictators. Dictatorship is the only way in which government can accomplish anything. See what a mess democracy has led to. Why are you afraid of dictatorship?"

The last six years under President Trump (4) and President Biden (2) our democracy has been a mess: deep divisions, chaos, and full of loathing hatred for each other. The country desperately needs a drastic change in leadership to restore unity, respect, and hopefully, a common vision that does not include former President Trump or present President Biden as the Commander-in-Chief.

Sincerely in the Risen Lord,

Fr. Tom Heron

This letter expressed my concern over the moral and civic disarray in American leadership. It was a plea for unity, clarity, and a vision beyond partisan extremes.

As Catholics, we are all called to be the voice for the voiceless, and I feel this responsibility keenly. As St. John's Gospel reminds us, Jesus came that we might have life and have it in abundance.[15] That promise applies to every human being, born and unborn. Biden, like all of us, is called to align his life with the Gospel's wisdom and truth. Yet his public actions suggest otherwise. Archbishop Wilton Gregory once referred to him as a "cafeteria Catholic,"[16] a term that stings not because it is harsh but because it is accurate. One cannot selectively follow Christ's teachings without distorting the Gospel's integrity.

This is not about Democrats versus Republicans; it's about human dignity. Both Presidents Biden and Trump have failed to model what it means to be good humans and good Americans. Their public behavior often falls far short of the moral standard we need from our leaders. The commandment "Thou shalt not kill" and the Hippocratic Oath to "do no harm" are not partisan principles, but universal truths. When Biden claims that his policies reflect compassion, I challenge him to consider whether true compassion can ever involve the destruction of innocent lives.

THE COST OF CONVICTION

Writing letters of opinion is not for the faint of heart. It requires courage, humility, and a willingness to face criticism. But it is also a way of living out the Gospel, of bringing light to dark places, and of speaking for those who cannot speak for themselves. Let us never underestimate the power of words to heal, to challenge, and to bring people closer to the truth. Every letter we write is a sacred echo of our faith, calling out into the world: "Here I am. Send me" (Isaiah 6:8).

We will now venture into the science of writing within one's own vocation. Before we depart this topic, however, I leave you with these words from St. Paul.

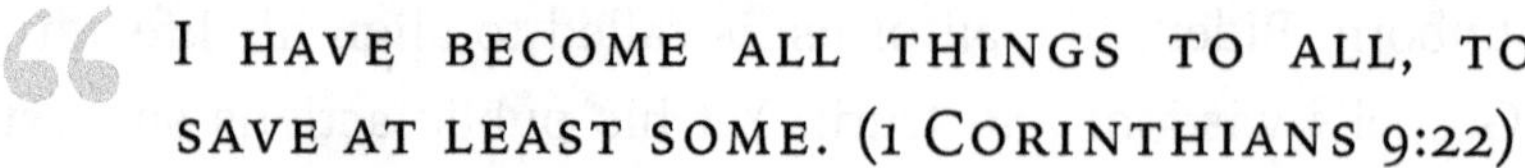

> I HAVE BECOME ALL THINGS TO ALL, TO SAVE AT LEAST SOME. (1 CORINTHIANS 9:22)

Whether writing to a newspaper editor, a politician, or a grieving family, my goal has always been the same: to share the love of Christ in a world that so desperately needs it.

CHAPTER 4

The Collar and the Cross

LETTERS OF TRUTH AND TENSION IN THE PRIESTHOOD

I've experienced the joy of thoughtfully exchanging letters with my fellow clergymen throughout my vocation of more than forty years as a priest. In some cases, the letters are bright with a tone of friendliness and positivity, which often stems from a positive encounter I had with that individual. I would try to write to say how much I enjoyed our meeting or collaboration.

Other times, I'd use the term "serious" as the tone, rather than diplomatic. The seriousness was to address miscommunication that needed further voicing. In those letters, I may write with forcefulness in order to get the point across that may have been neglected in a prior exchange.

As you've seen in the letters I've shared thus far, I am a strong proponent of "macros," or in other words, impactful quotes to supplement the content. I maintain a database of more than 600 of these macros ... pages and pages of them! There is a universal wisdom throughout written history that can be applied to a specific situation. Although he had passed decades before Jesus's ministry, the influence of Horace's literary work was still very much alive.[17] His odes were craftily composed to spread wisdom. I quote Horace to bring that knowledge from the past to the present day in the content of my letters. It's enriching to the recipient. I think they are a nice touch, as I've said what I've said, but this person's words can confirm exactly what I'm saying.

I always felt that forthrightness was lacking among priest-to-priest exchanges. I've confronted seminarians, I've confronted three priests and a bride, and I've confronted the archdiocese (more on that in the next chapter). However, I never resorted to letter writing without first approaching those individuals face-to-face. We would sit down and discuss what was happening. I wanted to be enlightened if I was misreading the situation. I'm very receptive to that. Many times, however, I would be met with defensiveness and anger rather than a healthy debate.

SEEKING SERENITY: A FRIEND'S CALL TO ACTION

In the crucible of my pastoral challenges at St. James Parish, where hostility and division threatened to unravel the very fabric of our community, there came a moment of profound grace: a letter from Father Fran Meehan to Monsignor Dan Sullivan. It was not addressed to me directly, but it was for me in every sense of the word a powerful affirmation of support during one of the most turbulent chapters of my priesthood.

Father Fran Meehan was no ordinary theologian. He was a luminary in moral theology, a professor who had taught both Monsignor Sullivan and me in the seminary. Respected not only for his intellectual brilliance but also for his deep humility,

Father Meehan was a man who could distill the most complex situations into a call for fairness, reconciliation, and truth. His words, whether spoken in the classroom or written in a letter, carried the weight of wisdom, and his calming presence was a balm for many who sought his counsel.

Msgr Dan Sullivan

Dear Dan,
I hope your summer is going well and that you do get some time. I wanted to write this note to you regarding Father Tom Heron. Please pardon my taking the way of email, when a note of such seriousness as this one probably should rise above the genre of email.

Tom spoke to me today. Once in a while he speaks with me, --not in any formal relationship of spiritual direction as such, but just as to someone who helps.

Tom recounted all that has transpired over this year. He is, by the way, extremely grateful to you for your understanding and goodness to him. So be sure that this letter does not come as a form of advocacy, nor is it written in any way as an effort to infuence you.

On the contrary, it is more to thank you, and simply to encourage you in your own positive way of being a help to Tom. Sometimes, when we are in authority, - even as I was in a parish - it helps to have someone ratify what already are our instincts; and that is the purpose of this note.

That is, I simply wish to communicate to you my own conviction (added to yours), that Tom has truly suffered huge injustices, unconscionable hostility, shocking defamation, false accusation - all of which seem to have risen to a level of real evil. Sometimes when a good priest is defamed in such a dramatic way, I begin to wonder about demonic forces. By this you understand, I am sure, that I do not accuse Tom's accusers of being demonic people, but simply that a spirit can set in that is an instrument of the demonic - no matter how unconscious and unknowing such a dynamic might be within the individual people involved.

So, I simply write this note, Dan, to affirm what seems to be your own conviction as well as your way of supporting and helping Tom. Thank you for your kindness in catching the spirit of this note; and always a thank you for your goodness in working with the dfficult discernments always involved in parish conflicts.

Warm best wishes,
Sincerely yours,
Fran Meehan

This private note, shared here with permission, was a great consolation during a season of trial. It reminded me that even amid false accusation and pain, grace finds its way through the compassion and discernment of others.

By the time Father Meehan wrote his letter in June 2010, I had already met with Monsignor Sullivan to discuss the escalating tensions at St. James. Swastikas had been scrawled on the parish buildings, school, pre-school, Church, and rectory in yellow paint. Anonymous mobs gathered in parking lots during parish council meetings, and verbal assaults were hurled my way, sometimes even within the sacred walls of the church. One man, in a moment of unbridled rage, swung at me after I had just celebrated Mass and was greeting people as they made their way to the parking lot. He blamed me for everything he believed I had ruined: the parish, the school, and even the neighborhood. The breaking point for many of these individuals seemed to be my decision to lease the parish school building to a Jewish group. In a community like Elkins Park, where the population was substantially Jewish, I saw this as an opportunity to build bridges. But to some, it was an unforgivable betrayal.

I had sought Father Meehan's guidance during this time, not to shift the burden of leadership but to ensure I was navigating these troubled waters with pastoral and moral clarity. His response, however, was unexpected. Instead of writing to me, he chose to write to Monsignor Sullivan, a man who had already shown his unwavering support for my efforts. Fran's letter was not one of advocacy, as he was careful to clarify, but one of affirmation for both Dan and me. It was a call to encourage, to uplift, and to reinforce the conviction that we were striving for justice and reconciliation in a deeply fractured community.

In his letter, Father Meehan described the "unconscionable hostility, shocking defamation, and false accusation" I had endured, going so far as to suggest that such behavior bordered on the demonic. Yet, Father Meehan, in his characteristic fairness, did not accuse my detractors of being evil people. Rather, he identified a dangerous spirit at work, one that could infiltrate even the most unassuming hearts and sow discord where there should be unity.

What struck me most about Father Meehan's words was their gentleness. Even as he acknowledged the severity of the situation, he framed his observations with humility and grace. "Sometimes," he wrote, "when we are in authority, even as I was in a parish, it helps to have someone ratify what already are our instincts." His message to Monsignor Sullivan was clear: Stand firm in your support for Tom, because the path he is walking is not an easy one, but it is the right one.

Reading Father Meehan's letter reminded me of the central lesson from the chapter "Pastor Again" in my first book, *We Are All Called*. During that difficult time at St. James, I learned that being a pastor meant standing in the breach, absorbing the anger, misunderstanding, and even hatred that could arise when trying to shepherd a divided flock. It was not about self-defense or self-preservation; it was about being a bridge, a living conduit for God's grace, even when it felt like the bridge might buckle under the weight.

Father Meehan's letter also carried a subtle but profound wisdom about the nature of advocacy. It was not about taking sides or inflaming tensions. It was about seeing the humanity in everyone involved, even those who sought to tear you down. Father Meehan's approach was not to vilify but to clarify, to help others see the broader picture, and to guide them toward a resolution that honored truth and love.

There is a macro I often rely on in moments like these, a quote by Dr. Martin Luther King that I have kept close to my heart:

"Injustice anywhere is a threat to justice everywhere."[18] Father Meehan's letter exemplified this truth. He saw the injustices I faced not as isolated incidents but as part of a larger pattern that demanded attention and action. His words were a lifeline, a reminder that even in the darkest moments, there are those who will stand with you, who will speak truth to power, and who will call forth the best in all of us, even when it seems buried beneath layers of pain and prejudice.

In many ways, Father Meehan's letter to Monsignor Sullivan was not just a note of encouragement; it was a call to action for anyone who reads it, myself included. It asked us to rise above the pettiness of divisive rhetoric and to hold fast to the principles of our faith that demand courage, compassion, and a commitment to the truth. For me, it served as a reminder of why I chose this vocation in the first place: to be a shepherd, even when the wolves are at the gate.

Reflecting on Father Meehan's words now, I am struck by their enduring relevance. We live in a time when hostility and misunderstanding often dominate public discourse and when the impulse to tear down often outweighs the desire to build up. Father Meehan's letter is a testament to the power of thoughtful, measured words to cut through the noise and offer a path toward healing and reconciliation.

For all his wisdom and brilliance, Father Fran Meehan never sought the spotlight. He was, in the best sense, a quiet giant. He was a man whose presence was felt not through volume but through depth. His letter to Monsignor Dan Sullivan stands as a powerful example of how even a single voice, spoken with clarity and love, can make a difference. It is a voice I carry with me still, a voice that echoes the very heart of what it means to be a priest: to speak not for oneself but for the One who calls us to be instruments of peace in a world so desperately in need of it.

A LIFETIME OFFER OF MUTUAL SUPPORT

The Philadelphia priesthood has always been a complex tapestry of camaraderie and competition, fraternity and friction. In the midst of it, bonds are formed, some fleeting and others lasting. My relationship with Bishop Michael Burbidge, now shepherding the Diocese of Arlington in Virginia, is one such immovable bond, and a connection forged in shared experiences and mutual respect.

Mike and I entered the seminary around the same time, me in 1970 and he in 1975. From our first days together as students, we seemed to find ourselves walking parallel paths. Both of us had pastoral assignments in large parishes, both of us taught high school, and both of us were later assigned to the seminary's formation faculty. These shared experiences bred a natural friendship strengthened by our shared roots in Delaware County. We're both dyed-in-the-wool Eagles fans, raised in similar neighborhoods and steeped in the same traditions. He attended Cardinal O'Hara High School, as I attended Msgr. Bonner High School. Later, he even taught at O'Hara, much like my own teaching days.

Mike's rise within the Church was meteoric, a testament to his natural gifts and the esteem in which he was held by Cardinal Anthony Bevilacqua. As Bevilacqua's secretary, Mike became a trusted confidant and protégé, earning the cardinal's unwavering admiration. So much so, in fact, that when Bevilacqua named him a bishop—a mere eighteen years after Mike's priesthood ordination—many priests in Bevilacqua's inner circle were left stunned, perhaps even envious. It was a reminder of the human dimensions of priestly fraternity, where ambition and disappointment often coexist with humility and grace.

MOST REVEREND MICHAEL F. BURBIDGE
BISHOP OF RALEIGH

February 19, 2014

Dear ~~Father Heron~~, Tom,

Thank you for your thoughtful letter and for the Mass you will offer for my beloved mother. My family and I are most grateful. Please know that I also deeply appreciate your fraternal support, especially at this time.

Be assured of my continued prayers for you and your beloved mother. May Our Lord Jesus bless you with the gift of His peace now and always.

Fraternally in Christ,

Mike

Thanks so much for your comforting words, prayers + fraternal support. Most grateful Tom!

MOST REVEREND MICHAEL F. BURBIDGE
BISHOP OF RALEIGH
January 13, 2015

Dear Tom,

Thank you for the thoughtful letter you sent me and for your prayerful remembrance of my beloved mother. I am most grateful for your kindness and fraternal support.

Please be assured of my continued prayers for you and your intentions. May Our Lord Jesus bless you with the gift of His peace throughout the New Year and always.

Fraternally in Christ,

Mike

I continue to pray for our beloved Dan and ask for his intercession.

Eagles in 2015!!

These notes from Bishop Burbidge reflect the quiet beauty of fraternal priestly friendship, grounded in prayer, grief, humor, and a shared hope in the Lord.

But what I've always admired about Mike is his capacity for gratitude and mutual support. The letters he wrote to me in 2014 and 2015, though brief, are characteristic of him. They speak of appreciation and prayer, of the bond we share as brothers in Christ. His words were a response to my own small gesture: a letter offering condolences for the loss of his beloved mother and the promise of a Mass celebrated in her memory. A year later, he reiterated his gratitude, adding, "I continue to pray for our beloved Dan and ask for his intercession," talking about my dear spiritual director, Monsignor Dan Murray.

That's the thing about Mike. He never lets kindness go unanswered. He has a way of acknowledging even the simplest acts of support, making you feel that your effort, however small, truly matters. It's a rare quality, even among priests, to respond with such sincerity and warmth.

Still, I can't ignore the undercurrents of rivalry and resentment that sometimes surface in the Philadelphia priesthood. Mike's appointment as bishop undoubtedly stirred those waters, as did many other promotions and assignments over the years. I've seen firsthand how the weeds and wheat grow together within our ranks. The bonds of fraternity are real, but so too are the fractures: petty grievances, bruised egos, and the ever-present temptation to measure one's worth against another's success.

In reflecting on my friendship with Mike, I'm reminded of the importance of focusing not on titles or accolades but on the shared mission that binds us as priests. Each of us is called to shepherd God's people, to preach the Gospel, and to bear witness to Christ's love. Whether as pastors, teachers, or bishops, our true worth lies not in the roles we play but in the faithfulness with which we live out our calling.

Mike's letters to me, simple as they may seem, are a testament to that faithfulness. They remind me that even in the midst of human frailty and institutional politics, there is a higher calling that unites us. His prayers for me, for my intentions, and for our mutual friends like Dan Murray, are a reflection of the enduring support that should define the priesthood. And for that, I am humbly grateful.

A DEEPER CONNECTION

Writing to Bishop Bob Morneau has always felt like a privilege, a moment of rekindling a connection with someone whose life has been a testament to the harmony of intellect, humility, and faith. Our friendship began years ago, during a course on priestly formation at Seton Hall, where he served as a lecturer. Poetry was our initial meeting ground. Bob has an almost unbelievable ability to recite nearly 3,000 poems from memory, a gift that speaks not just to his intellect but to his deep love for the beauty of words and the truths they carry.

It wasn't long before our shared passions extended beyond poetry. Whether it was playing basketball or tennis, Bob's zest for life was infectious. He had an uncanny way of bringing a sense of joy and camaraderie to whatever we were doing. On the tennis court, you'd see his competitive streak tempered by his characteristically kind demeanor. Every match was a reflection of his personality: humble, unpretentious, yet deeply engaging.

Bob is a man of great gifts, both intellectual and spiritual. Ordained a bishop in his 30s—an extraordinary feat—his early rise was a testament to his abilities and character. Yet, despite the grandeur of his position, Bob has always lived simply. His diet, his demeanor, and his way of life reflected an ascetic quality. At lunch, he'd order half a sandwich or a cup of soup, never more than what he needed. He approached the world with a remarkable balance of wisdom and humility, grounded in his faith.

One of the most moving aspects of Bob's life was his decision to step down from active ministry, a choice that spoke volumes about his integrity. Early in his episcopacy, he addressed a situation involving a priest accused of inappropriate conduct. Bob mediated a resolution, extracting a promise from the priest never to engage in such behavior again. When, decades later, that promise was broken, Bob felt he had failed the family and his calling. His resignation was not a public display of guilt but a private act of conscience. It was an extraordinary gesture of accountability and humility. I don't think there is another bishop in the world who would have done what Bob did. His decision reflects a moral courage that is all too rare.

I've always admired Bob's ability to elevate those around him. His conversations, no matter how brief, had a lasting impact. A three-minute exchange with Bob could linger in your mind for days, stirring new reflections and insights. He had a knack for admonishing and instructing with grace, embodying St. Paul's exhortation to "admonish one another."[19] He never lorded his authority over others but lived out his role as a bishop with the heart of a father. For younger priests, he was a source of encouragement and fraternity, modeling what it means to be a shepherd in the truest sense.

November 10, 2022

Bishop Robert Morneau

Dear Bob,

I am thrilled that we finally reconnected. Your humor is as strong as ever. To me, that is a sign of a robust life, especially regarding tennis and the Packers.

I have enclosed a poem, a book, and a letter that I wrote to a remarkable doctor who is laser-focused on healing all of his patients. I am fortunate to be counted as one of his patients.

A joyful, blessed Thanksgiving to you, Bishop Banks, and your family.

"Don't just love, astonish people with your love. Don't just dabble in generosity, live a life of staggering generosity."

(Matthew Kelly)

In Corde Christi,

Tom

This note to Bishop Morneau was more than a seasonal greeting. It was a celebration of resilience, humor, and the sacred joy of old friendships rekindled.

In my letter to Bob, I enclosed a poem, a book, and a letter I had written to a remarkable doctor. I knew Bob would appreciate these gifts not as mere tokens but as reflections of the deep bond we share. He has always had a way of receiving words with the same care and intention with which they are offered. When I share my writing with Bob, I know it will be met with a heartfelt response, one that carries the weight of mutual respect and understanding.

In our correspondence, I quoted Matthew Kelly: "Don't just love, astonish people with your love. Don't just dabble in generosity, live a life of staggering generosity."[20] This quote encapsulates what Bob has modeled throughout his life: a love and generosity that astonishes because they come from a place of genuine humility and faith.

To know Bob is to experience a deeper connection, one that enriches your life and inspires you to be better. He embodies the ideal of a bishop, not in regalia or position, but in spirit and action. Writing to him is more than an exchange of words; it is a continuation of a friendship rooted in faith, love, and a shared commitment to the Gospel. It is an affirmation that in the communion of saints, even across distance, we are united in purpose and prayer.

As I think of Bob, I am reminded of the words of St. Paul: "Your every act should be done with love" (1 Corinthians 16:14). Bob has lived this out in his ministry, his friendships, and his life. It is a lesson I carry with me and one I hope to emulate in my own vocation.

CORRESPONDENCE ROOTED IN HILARITY

As a young boy, six or seven years old, due largely to my mother's lively faith and Christ-like example, I was fascinated with the idea that the goal of every person is to be a saint.

In 1989, I met a priest, Father William McNamara, who captured the essence of a saint in two words: "touched sinner." We are all sinners, and despite our sinfulness, we are all called to be saints and we can never forget that truth; however, we all need to be set free from all patterns of sinful living, pride, greed, fear, lust, dishonesty; and that happens when Jesus touches us with His abundant grace, His life and love.

Father William McNamara was unlike anyone I'd ever encountered. I first met him in the summer of 1989 at Seton Hall University. He was a guest lecturer, and I was there for a course on priestly formation. His very first conference had me falling out of my chair with laughter. He possessed a rare wit that reminded me of my grandfather, and believe me, that is the highest compliment I could offer anyone. My grandfather had a knack for finding humor in the most unexpected moments, and so did Father William. His observations on life, faith, and humanity were not only uproariously funny but also deeply insightful.

Father William and I shared an immediate connection. Over the years, I visited him in various hermitages: Nova Scotia, Crestone, Colorado, Sedona, Arizona, and Skreen, Ireland. Each location bore his signature touch: a simple, natural environment meant to draw one closer to God through solitude, silence, and stillness. He believed these three conditions were essential for fostering a healthy solidarity with others. He would often say that the noise pollution of our modern lives stifles our ability to truly connect with God, with ourselves, and with each other. And he practiced what he preached. Every retreat at his hermitages was a lesson in simplicity: sparse food, a small hut for each retreatant, and breathtaking natural beauty that forced you to confront your smallness in the vastness of creation.

In Crestone, Colorado, the hermitage overlooked the Sangre de Christo, a mountain range so majestic it brought new meaning to the idea of going up to the mountaintop to rejoice! Father William used to say that Jesus's own practice of retreating to the mountains, the desert, or the lakeside wasn't just about solitude. It was preparation. Jesus entered the stillness to pray and renew His strength so He could face the brokenness of the human condition with healing power. Father William believed this same practice was vital for priests today.

September 26, 2005

Letter from Father William to Father Heron:

Tom:

Thank you! Your gift helps enormously. It was bracing to see you and share a bit with you.

The rest of the trip went well. Am now packing for Oregon. Am thrilled to be going there and living alone (al-one). The manual labor will be a challenge. The solitude and silence sheer joy.

Great to see you in action! You radiate pastoral aplomb. I'll be at Corpus Christi Hermitage, New Pine Creek, Oregon 97635 (Kelly Creek Road). Soon I'll have a P.O. Box and an emergency phone.

Bless me,
William

p.s.: Esalen just informed me it is my responsibility to promote "The Big Sun Seminar" first weekend of December on *The Future of the Church*. But I'll be in solitude until then. Could you announce it?

p.p.s.: I'll send a template when I get it. Crestone won't share the list I built up over 40 years. (Come, Holy Spirit!)

In this note, Father William shares his joy in entering deeper solitude, where manual labor and silence become sacraments. His words affirm the fruitfulness of priestly friendship and the mutual joy of serving in Christ.

In his letter to me dated Sept. 26, 2005 (the handwriting was always atrocious, so I spared you, the reader, by transcribing it), Father William captured his unique blend of humor and spiritual wisdom. He was preparing to live alone in a hermitage in Oregon, embracing manual labor and solitude with an almost childlike glee. “Manual labor will be a challenge,” he wrote. But he saw it not as a burden but as sheer joy. That was Father William—a man who found the divine even in the humblest of tasks. His humor shone through in every line, even in his closing: “Bless me.” It wasn’t just a plea for prayer but a lighthearted reminder of the sacredness in our shared humanity.

Father William had a phrase for what he believed a priest should be: an "earthy mystic." It’s a paradox that captures the essence of his spirituality. To be earthy is to be grounded in humility, fully aware of our humanity and limitations. To be mystic is to strive for holiness, to reflect the face of Christ in all that we do. He taught me that these two aspects must be held in balance. Too much earthiness, and we risk losing sight of our divine calling. Too much mysticism, and we risk becoming detached from the very people we are called to serve.

His influence on me was profound. It was through my friendship with Father William that I developed what I call the "4H Club”: humility, hilarity, hospitality, and holiness. Humility reminds us that we are no better than those we serve. Hilarity ensures we don’t take ourselves too seriously. Hospitality welcomes people in their brokenness, enabling holiness to grow in both priest and parishioner.

May 14, 1999

Dear Fr. William,

It was a joy to speak with you on the phone. I am still saddened by your present circumstances. I shall continue to remember you and all the members of Nada and Holy Hill in my prayers. It is my deep hope that this tragedy will somehow end in reunited comedy.

Pray for me.

Sincerely in Our Lord,

Fr. Tom Heron

Dear Fr. William, It was a joy to speak with you on the phone. I am still saddened by your present circumstances. I shall continue to remember you and all the members of Nada and Holy Hill in my prayers. It is my deep hope that this tragedy will somehow end in reunited comedy. Pray for me. Sincerely in Our Lord, Fr. Tom Heron

In a letter I wrote to him in May 1999, I sought to encourage him during a particularly difficult time in his life. He had been accused of priestly misconduct with adult women—a charge I found wholly lacking in credibility—and had stepped down from leadership in his community. Father William was a man of integrity, deeply committed to truth and justice. Even in the face of false accusations, he bore his cross with grace. I remember telling him that I would continue to pray for him and for the community he had served so faithfully. It was my hope, I wrote, that "this tragedy will somehow end in reunited comedy."

Father William was one of those rare souls who could turn even the heaviest of burdens into an opportunity for growth. He taught me that laughter is a form of grace, a way of lifting the soul out of despair. His life was a testament to the power of joy, humility, and faith. And though he is no longer with us, his legacy lives on in the countless lives he touched, including mine.

Father William's teachings on solitude, silence, and stillness have stayed with me. They remind me that the priesthood is not just about serving others but also about nurturing one's own relationship with God. His humor and humility taught me to find joy in the journey, even in the face of adversity. And his friendship showed me the true meaning of fraternity, one rooted not in titles or positions but in a shared commitment to Christ.

I am reminded of his favorite phrase: "Don't lose your capacity to be surprised." It's a call to remain open to the unexpected ways God works in our lives, a call I strive to live out every day.

IN INK AND SPIRIT

Flannery O'Connor is often attributed for saying, "I write because I don't know what I think until I read what I say."[21] Writing demands clarity. It compels us to wrestle with our beliefs, to weigh them in the light of truth, and to present them with humility. Each letter, whether written to a bishop, a friend, or a fellow priest, is a step toward understanding, both of the recipient and of myself. Through ink and paper, we uncover the mystery of human connection and the grace that flows through it.

Letters are not always received with warmth or understanding. The same pen that fosters connection can also pierce the heart when addressing conflict. How do we navigate the tensions that arise when convictions collide? How do we write not to alienate but to illuminate? These are the questions we will explore, knowing that even in conflict, the goal remains the same: to reflect the face of Christ in all that we do. Let us step forward together, ready to embrace the challenge of writing truth with love.

CHAPTER 5

In the Trenches

CONFRONTING CONFLICT WITH COURAGE

In the previous chapter, we explored the ministry of letters as a means of fostering fraternity, offering encouragement, and deepening spiritual bonds. Yet, not every letter carries the fragrance of mutual respect or shared understanding. Some, instead, bear the weight of conflict: letters written in the heat of tension, amidst misunderstandings, or in response to manipulations that cut to the quick. These letters are no less an expression of my priesthood, though they often demand a different kind of grace: the courage to confront, the wisdom to temper firm truths with charity, and the commitment to remain anchored in integrity.

Conflict is inevitable in any vocation, but within the priesthood, it often feels particularly sharp. The Church is a human institution, and like any such institution, it is vulnerable to the very frailties it seeks to redeem. Misunderstandings arise, egos collide, and factions form. Letters become necessary in these moments, not as weapons but as instruments of clarity, seeking to pierce through the fog of division and bring to light the

Gospel's call to reconciliation. These are the moments when the medium, as Marshall McLuhan once said, becomes the message.[22] The words themselves may carry the argument, but the tone, the intention, and the spirit behind them must carry the weight of truth.

Writing in times of conflict is walking a tightrope. There is always the temptation to wield words like a hammer, to crush the opposition with sharp retorts and unyielding arguments. I have often found myself staring at a blank page, wrestling with that very impulse. It is easy to forget, in moments of frustration, that the person on the other side of the letter is not simply an adversary but a soul in need of grace. And yet, I must balance that with the knowledge that I cannot allow myself—or the truth I represent—to be trampled. Finding that equilibrium requires prayer, discernment, and a commitment to be forceful without being destructive, to illuminate rather than annihilate.

Conflict letters require a particular kind of tone; firm, yes, but also measured and unambiguous. There is no room for ambiguity when addressing manipulation, dishonesty, or injustice. I recall a series of exchanges with a fellow priest, whose letters I read as nothing short of calculated manipulation. His tone sought to disarm me, presenting a veneer of camaraderie while attempting to steer me into decisions that suited his purposes alone. I knew I had to respond, not with equal cunning, but with clarity and strength. To confront manipulation with silence is to condone it. To confront it with truth is to disrupt its power.

There is no denying the emotional toll these letters can take. Writing them requires stepping into the tension and holding it long enough to discern the best path forward. When I sit down to write such a letter, I am keenly aware of the responsibility it carries. Words have the power to heal or to harm, to build bridges, or to burn them. In moments of conflict, I must remind myself that my goal is not to win an argument but to reflect the face of Christ. That requires humility, restraint, and a willingness to listen even as I speak.

As we step into the trenches of the conflicts that follow, I invite you to consider the lessons they hold, not just for priests but for anyone navigating the complexities of human relationships. How do we confront manipulation without losing our own integrity? How do we address division while remaining rooted in charity? And how do we write letters that speak not just to the situation at hand but to the deeper truths that transcend it?

GOOD SHEPHERD – CONFRONTING THE UNRAVELING OF COMMUNITY BONDS

When I arrived at Good Shepherd Parish in 1998, it was clear that I was stepping into a delicate, fracturing situation. Once a flourishing and tightly knit Catholic community, the parish had witnessed decades of slow and steady decline. The neighborhood, marked by economic hardship and a shifting demographic, mirrored the parish's struggles. What had once been a vibrant, homogenous congregation of white families was now a mosaic of cultures: a growing Asian Catholic community, a significant Liberian population, and the remnants of the original Irish and Italian families who had built the parish in the early 20th century.

The church itself became a symbolic reflection of the divisions. During Sunday Mass, the Blessed Mother side of the church was often populated by the white "old guard," the St. Joseph side was claimed by the Asian community, and the Liberian families filled the middle and back pews. Despite my efforts to foster unity—changing the way Communion was distributed to encourage mingling and hosting coffee-and-donut gatherings after Mass—the separation was palpable. Resistance to change became a recurring theme. One lifelong parishioner whose family's ties to the parish stretched back generations voiced her discontent over even minor adjustments. She wasn't alone.

From the outset, challenges came fast and unrelenting. The parish school was on the brink of closure, a casualty of plummeting enrollment. Of the 170 children still attending, only a dozen were Catholic. Financial instability loomed large, and the once-thriving school was a shadow of its former self. For many longtime parishioners, the school's demise was a painful reminder of what they perceived as the loss of their parish's identity. However, they were unwilling to confront the harsh reality that the Catholic population in the neighborhood had diminished to a point of no return.

I committed myself to the community. I walked the streets, visited families, and engaged with schools in the area, including the public school across the street from the parish. Yet, these efforts were not met with universal approval. A small but vocal contingent of parishioners criticized me at every turn. They held me personally responsible for the parish's decline that had been decades in the making, long before my arrival.

October 28, 1999

Rev. Thomas Herron

Dear Father Herron:

For quite some time I have tried to determine how to help Good Shepard. I battled frustration with the apparent loss of life and spirit within the parish. It was quite easy to lay much of the blame at your feet. Obviously being new, a clear representative of change, made you a bold target. I, like others, focused on how you did things differently - and as such, the wrong way. I struggled with jumping on the bandwagon of criticism of which I am sure you are aware.

My family has been involved with Good Shepard since before the church was even built. My Grandfather literally helped to build and maintain the church, school, rectory and convent. My Dad grew up across the street from the church. My Aunt, devoted years of voluntary service to the financial administration of the parish.

But perhaps more importantly, Good Shepard was a place of comfort when I, after years of rejecting God, recognized my faith and began to attend church again. I literally felt compelled to attend Mass at Good Shepard, mostly likely because of the family connection. Good Shepard is a clear reminder of my renewed faith. For that reason, I want to continue to be a part of the parish.

I have come to believe that the future of the parish is in our collective hands. We need to work together to strengthen our faith, spirit and commitment. I am confident that you are aware of the actions you have taken which have contributed to the loss of spirit. At the same time,

This letter exhibits the passion that can exist in a long-standing parish community…

Page Two

I am confident that our parish is a faithful community which will recognize the need to put aside past differences to focus on the future health of Good Shepard.

I recognize that you may well feel under siege. You might also feel perplexed why such an obviously faithful community has seemed to give up, join in useless criticism, withdrawn from helping the parish flourish. Such feeling would clearly be justified. Yet, I am confident that you could lead the parish toward a change in spirit. There is simply no underestimating the respect parishioners have for you as Pastor.

Please consider some strategy/action which would promote healing within the parish. I know that personal differences with you have alienated some parishioners from our community. Please consider some reconciliation toward those folks individually as well as for the entire parish. Again, you have the power to lead by example. And I remain confident that parishioners will follow.

Finally, please understand that this letter was a difficult undertaking. Frankly, it would have been easier to complain to the Vicar. But I want to help the parish. Going to the Vicar will not accomplish that goal, as demonstrated by those who have made such complaints. Rather, it is necessary that we recognize our failings, forgive past hostilities, and embrace a future of working together with respect.

I sincerely hope that you will consider these thoughts - the future of Good Shepard is in your hands.

If you would like to discuss these issues, please feel free to contact me. I would really appreciate the opportunity to talk to you if you think that I can be helpful.

Peace,

…and its author was fixated on the golden years that were dwindling in a church community that wasn't quite what it once was.

One parishioner, in particular, wielded her pen with fervor, sending me letters that oscillated between expressing her deep ties to the parish and lambasting my leadership. In her correspondence, she lamented the “loss of spirit” within the parish and implored me to return Good Shepherd to its former glory. Her frustration often boiled over into thinly veiled accusations that I was unfit for the role of pastor. She refused to acknowledge the parish's structural and demographic challenges, insisting instead that my leadership—or lack thereof—was to blame.

Her sister was equally vocal in her discontent. During one particularly contentious Sunday Mass, she took it upon herself to address the congregation without my permission, disparaging my efforts and questioning my motives. Her disruption forced me to act decisively. After the Mass, I asked her not to attend the next service, and eventually, I removed her from the Parish Council. This decision, though necessary, only fueled her animosity. She wrote letters to Church leadership, painting herself as a victim of my supposed authoritarian leadership. In her eyes, my refusal to capitulate to her demands was proof of my unworthiness.

December 6, 2001

Dear Sister

I regret to inform you that Father Heron has removed me from the Pastoral Council.

On Sunday, December 2nd, at the 7:30 Mass after introducing Disciples in Mission, I proceeded to give the congregation an update on the activities of the Pastoral Council and the Save Our School Committee. The following is what I said:

> "The S.O.S. Committee met with Father Heron, Sister and and laid out our plans for keeping the school open hoping Father would reverse his decision. Father informed us he has not changed his mind and will submit the Viability Study to the Vicar and the Cardinal to close Good Shepherd".

Father approached me after mass and told me I should not have made this announcement. He was upset that I had not mentioned my plans to make this announcement. I explained I was not aware the information given to the Steering Committee was not to be made public and all I did was tell the people Father had not changed his mind. The process of going to the Monsignor and then on to the Cardinal was explained to us at the meeting in the Spring when the recommendation was announced. A heated exchange followed, with me promising not to repeat the announcement when I returned to introduce Disciples in Mission at the at the 11:00 mass.

On Tuesday evening after the Disciples in Mission gathering Father informed me he was removing me from the Pastoral Council, the Cluster and I am prohibited from speaking on anything other than Disciples in Mission from the pulpit..

An attempt was made on my behalf and for the sake of the parish to see if Father would sit down with me, discuss the situation and see if cooler heads would prevail. It seems those efforts were to no avail.

Know that I will continue to work and support you in any way I can for the good of our dear Good Shepherd.

Sincerely yours,

This letter captures the deep strain that can arise in parish life when communication falters and emotions run high.

Through it all, I remained committed to the principles of pastoral leadership. I knew that a pastor must stand firm, even in the face of hostility. As I often reminded myself, the parable of the wheat and the weeds teaches us that there will be elements of division and discord in any community. Our task is not to uproot the weeds recklessly but to nurture the wheat, ensuring that the good can thrive despite the challenges.

The vicar for Philadelphia-South at the time played a peripheral but significant role in these conflicts. I reached out to him multiple times, seeking his support in addressing the tensions at Good Shepherd. Unfortunately, he declined my invitations to visit the parish, citing the potential reputational risks associated with becoming involved in such a volatile situation. His reluctance left me to navigate the storm largely on my own.

December 7, 2001

J.Thomas Heron

Dear Father Heron:

It is a sad day when a priest creates conflict instead of resolving it. The conflict with began when you became inflamed that she announced your intention to submit the feasibility study and closure recommendation to the Cardinal. You believed that had committed a violation of some rule. Nevertheless, at no point were we (Steering Committee members) asked to refrain from discussing your intention to submit the closure recommendation. In fact, in your letter to me on November 27, 2001, you requested that the information be shared with the Committee.

What offense was so great that a life-long member of the Parish be removed from her elected position to Pastoral Council? is so recognized by parishioners as a pillar of our church, she received the highest number of votes for election to the Council. Under what authority do you have to right to remove an elected member of the Council?

More importantly, what moral and professional obligation do you have to put your personal feelings aside and focus on what is best for Good Shepherd parish? I suggest it is a great obligation.

Good Shepherd Church is not ***your*** church. It belongs to all of us. You were not considering all of us when you removed from Council. You were only considering yourself.

Disagreement, dissent, and opposing views are simply part of life. They will not disappear because you cover your eyes and ears. The very clear message you are sending is that dissent will not be tolerated. While you can remove from Council, you can never take away the respect and admiration parishioners have for her.

Removing from the Pastoral Council smacks of rotaliation for her efforts to save Good Shepherd School from closure. After all, she simply re-stated what you had previously announced - that the school is closing.

A parishioner's letter of protest following my decision to remove a council member. The emotional stakes were high in the parish amid necessary school closures.

The financial scandals within the parish added another layer of complexity. A Sister and member of the IHM community who had served Good Shepherd since its founding was found to have embezzled more than $124,000 from school funds. Her actions not only betrayed the trust of the community but also further destabilized the already precarious financial situation. When I confronted her, she initially agreed to seek help, shedding crocodile tears as she promised to make amends. However, her actions spoke louder than her words, and the damage she inflicted on the parish's finances and morale was profound.

Despite the turmoil, there were moments of grace and growth. One of the most significant was the conversion of Fatima, a twelve-year-old Liberian girl raised by her mother and grandmother. In a parish where cultural divides often felt insurmountable, her journey to the Catholic faith was a testament to the power of God's grace to transcend barriers.

In my correspondence with the two sisters waging war against me at Good Shepherd, I sought to balance firmness with pastoral care. The former's letters often carried an undercurrent of nostalgia for a past that could not be reclaimed. She clung to the idea that Good Shepherd could somehow return to its glory days, refusing to accept the realities of the neighborhood's decline. In my responses, I acknowledged her pain and frustration but urged her to focus on the future rather than the past. I emphasized the need for the parish to adapt to its changing circumstances, to embrace the diversity within its pews, and to find new ways to live out its mission in the community.

January 25, 2002

Enclosed is a copy of the announcement you requested. I have also enclosed the announcement that appeared in Good Shepherd Sunday bulletin on January 13th.

Since the Save Our School Fund-raising Committee no longer exists, your request for the Committee to review the Feasibility/Closure recommendation would serve no fruitful purpose. This document was available from Sunday, November 24, 2001 until Sunday, January 13, 2002. I take this opportunity to thank (Pastoral Council Member), (Pastoral Council Member), (long-time parishioner), and (long-time parishioner) for their positive input on the Feasibility Study. I thank (Finance Council) and (Finance Council) for their input. Several other parishioners were invited to participate in the Feasibility Study process, for example, (a teacher) but for personal reasons declined. Finally, I express my gratitude to who once again demonstrated secretarial skills unsurpassed on this planet – the only person I ever met who can finish transcribing before I finish dictating.

I think it is time for all parishioners to accept the Cardinal's decision in a spirit of Christian charity and to dedicate our efforts to do all in our power to make Good Shepherd Parish a vibrant, faith community.

Sincerely in Our Lord,

J. Thomas Heron

Reverend J. Thomas Heron
Pastor

Dedicate yourselves to thankfulness. Let the word of Christ, rich as it is, dwell in you. In wisdom made perfect, instruct and admonish one another. Sing gratefully to God from your hearts in psalms, hymns, and inspired songs. Whatever you do, whether in speech or in action, do it in the name of the Lord Jesus. Give thanks to God the Father through Him.
Col 3: 14-17

After months of division and heartache, I wrote this letter to acknowledge those who offered constructive input and to encourage our community to turn the page, with renewed dedication to the life of the parish. My directness and tone are intentional.

With the latter, the approach was different. Her actions left little room for dialogue. When someone spits in your face and declares, "You're no priest," it becomes clear that their grievances are not merely about policy or leadership style. Her resistance was rooted in a fundamental refusal to see me as her pastor. In her letters, she suggested bringing in an outside mediator to resolve our conflict, a move I saw as a passive-aggressive attempt to undermine my authority. My response was direct but measured, reiterating my commitment to the parish and my responsibility as its pastor.

December 18, 2001

I acknowledge receipt of copies of your letters that you have sent to fellow parishioners and Cluster 33 board members regarding your removal from these committees. These letters were postmarked on December 14th and received by me on Monday, December 17th. I think it is necessary for me to respond to the various allegations you have made.

First, you have claimed that I do not understand your concern for the parishioners of Good Shepherd Parish. You have to understand that you are only one member of Good Shepherd Parish. Any number of people have voiced their concerns and shared their opinions with me ever since I was appointed pastor of Good Shepherd. Some of their concerns and their opinions disagree with yours. I listen to any concern and any opinion that a parishioner voices. With some, I agree, with others, I disagree. Whatever is best for the parish I try to do but you must understand that your vision of the parish cannot be the only valid opinion of what direction the parish should go.

Second, my decision to remove you from the Parish Pastoral Council and as sitting member of the Cluster Implementation Committee had absolutely nothing to do with the fact that I disagree with your opinion. My decision was based solely on the fact that you abused the use of the pulpit of Good Shepherd Parish. I was with you for 3-1/2 hours on Saturday, December 1st, at Saint Charles Seminary and you intentionally or unintentionally neglected to ask my permission to speak about the Parish Pastoral Council or the Save Our School Committee. In fact it is my recollection that rather than *asking* permission, you *informed* me that you would speak at both Masses the next day about Disciples in Mission. I gave you permission to speak on Disciples in Mission despite the fact that Sister Stella was already scheduled to speak for the Retirement Fund for Religious. Speaking on the other two topics, namely the Parish Pastoral Council and the Save Our School Committee, without permission constitutes an abuse of the pulpit. When I asked you why you didn't inform me, your response was that I would probably withhold this information from the people. I fail to see how you could come to that conclusion.

Through conflict, a letter oftentimes allows the opportunity to clarify position, intent, and/or a decision...

Letter to
December 18, 2001
Page Two

When I also informed you that no announcement from the pulpit about the status of Good Shepherd School could be made until I, as pastor, received an official response from Cardinal accepting or rejecting the Feasibility Study, your response was that you do not have to abide by such rules. By stating this you gave clear expression that you follow rules of your own making while ignoring the rules set by the Cardinal and by me as pastor. These are the reasons that you were removed from your position on the Parish Pastoral Council and the Cluster Implementation Committee.

Third, you claim that I have no authority to do this since you were elected by the people of the parish. Perhaps you do not understand the Canon Law of the church and the duties of the pastor of a parish when dealing with a parishioner who claims to be a rule unto herself.

Fourth, you state than an attempt was made on your behalf and for the sake of the parish (alluding to my telephone conversation with on December 6th) to see if I would sit down with you to discuss the situation and see if "clear heads would prevail." You further state that these efforts were to no avail. Since I told that I was willing to meet with you to discuss this situation, I fail to see how you came to that conclusion.

Fifth, your final comment to me was "you are no Christ." Obviously, your anger got the best of you. I find it puzzling that after reflecting and praying with the Disciples in Mission group for one hour on the readings of the First Sunday of Advent, especially from the book of the prophet Isaiah ***"they shall beat their swords into plowshares, and spears into pruning hooks,"*** you could make such a statement and with such venom.

By means of this letter I am clarifying my position and explaining to you my reasons for removing you from the Parish Pastoral Council and from the Cluster Implementation Committee. Your animosity toward me has made it impossible for you to work in a cooperative manner with me.

I would be willing to meet with you to discuss the contents of this letter. Let me know if are willing.

Sincerely in Our Lord,

J. Thomas Heron

Reverend J. Thomas Heron
Pastor

...and mine was to do what was best for Good Shepherd's parish community.

The challenges I faced at Good Shepherd were among the most difficult of my priesthood, but they were also among the most formative. They taught me the importance of resilience, the power of intentional communication, and the necessity of grace under pressure. Through it all, I held fast to the belief that even in the midst of conflict, there is an opportunity for growth for the parish, for its people, and for myself as their pastor.

A BATTLE FOR JUSTICE

The conflict over a disbanded church property is a tale of ecclesiastical negotiation laced with challenges that no seminary training could have prepared me for. When I became pastor of this parish community, the merger of neighboring parishes, including this property in particular, was well underway. Mergers always carry emotional weight. People mourn the loss of their beloved parishes, of their shared histories. But this situation was far more complex. It wasn't just about the practicalities of managing a merged parish; it was about facing entrenched entitlement, manipulative tactics, and a profound failure to uphold justice.

The issue at the heart of the debacle began with its canonical relegation, a process that stripped the property of its sacred designation. Canonically speaking, the property could then be sold or repurposed as needed. The sale of such properties is a delicate matter, fraught with the sensitivities of parishioners and the realities of diocesan oversight. But I had always approached these transactions with transparency and fairness, determined to ensure the best outcome for the parish and the greater Catholic community.

Enter a pastor whose intentions to acquire the property seemed, on the surface, sincere. However, as negotiations began, it became clear that sincerity was overshadowed by an overconfidence bolstered by his connections within the diocesan hierarchy. He was operating under the assumption that his ties to the archbishop's inner circle would shield him from accountability. The Fraternity offered $1.2 million for the property, far below its appraised value of $5.1 million at the time. It was an insult to the financial needs of the parish and to the principles of fair business practices.

Reverend J. Thomas Heron, Pastor Nov. 26, 2019

Dear Fr. Heron:

Thank you for your letter of Nov 18 concerning the Letter of Intent. I am sorry that you feel that "the appraiser's valuation of the property is incorrect and flawed." The appraisal was done by and it was reviewed by a few people in the commercial real estate business. They did not see any issues with it. I have included a copy of it for your review.

The appraisal was for $1.3 million. The offer was for $1.2 million because there has been a lot of work done to the property by the including work done by volunteers. Would you be able to supply copies of your appraisals for my files?

The was told that the sale would be based upon "as is" use. The fact that the property is valued at approximately $5,000,000 for "best use," should not really be brought into the discussion. As a result, referring to the "best use" valuation clouds the issue. For example:

- The office building cited in point 3 would impact the "best use" value, and not the "as is" use.
- In point 4 the letter mentions the "true value" of the church, and uses the sale of two churches The letter states that the "true value will only be established when we expose the property to the market through the competitive process to achieve the highest price for the asset." This is just is another way of bringing the "best use" value into the discussion.

In addition, it is important to remember that this is not a civil sale of the property, but only a canonical transfer of the property between two Archdiocesan entities. The sale will not entail any transfer of title, because all the property is held and will continue to be held bv the Archdiocese. The comparison to the sale of to the sale of is not accurate. Those were sales on the open market, as a result competitive forces were at work.

I am reminded of the Archbishop at our meeting last month on October 14, where the Archbishop spoke about his desire to save the church. He stressed that because it is a sacred site where the Mass will be offered, it should be saved. In addition, he said that in general he does not want to close churches and sell them, but would rather see them used as worship sites. Let us, then, work together to assure that remains a place where Our Lord is worshipped and honored.

In Christ,

In this letter, I sensed more than real estate concerns. I sensed politics cloaked in pastoral language. This was not just a transfer of property, but a tug-of-war over control, value, and the spiritual heartbeat of a church community.

My first letter to him was firm but measured. I appealed to the rhythm of the Church's liturgical life, using the Advent season as a metaphor for how we should approach all aspects of our lives, including contentious negotiations. Advent is a time of joyful anticipation, a season that calls us to prepare our hearts for the coming of Christ. I emphasized that even amidst tension, we must remain grounded in peace and gratitude. But I also made it abundantly clear that his offer was not only unreasonable but also insulting. "How is 'working together' now a priority," I wrote, "when you have been delinquent in paying rent for the last 15 months?" My language was direct, and perhaps some would say harsh, but it was necessary. Justice demanded clarity, not obfuscation.

December 2, 2019

Advent is an empty season – the quiet, still season when we refuse to be preoccupied with anything but the coming of Jesus. It is important to keep Advent as still and uncluttered as possible so that we will be awake and ready when Jesus comes. Advent cautions us against flirting with the fierce and fiery mystery of Jesus becoming man, of Jesus dwelling in our midst.

Joy is the characteristic Advent virtue. We are joyful during Advent because we experience the best of the past, present and future – all gathered together in an explosive moment of ecstasy. A calm faithful expectancy reigns in the Scriptures proclaimed, in this holy season, of child-like wonder and of hope in each of our hearts.

Thank you for your letter dated November 26, 2019. Your offer of 1.2 million for the entire property of as a canonical transfer is insufficient, unreasonable and unacceptable.

I was amused and puzzled by your call for us to "work together". How is "working together" a priority now, when you have been and continue to be delinquent in paying any rent to for the last 15 months? Both your lack of monthly rent payments and the offer of 1.2 million are short sighted and wrongheaded. Where is your sensible, honest cooperation regarding these two issues? Where is your sense of fairness, justice and decency? You seem completely uninterested to my attempts to give you a context and historical perspective of the past and present situation of in general and the Catholic community specifically.

So, let me be real clear; you, the Fraternity, the appraiser, or do not get to name the price for property. I do, in consultation with the Pastoral and Finance Councils of parish.

Regarding my appraisals...I shall share them with you once you have paid six month's rent to parish.

"But Jesus called them to him and said, "You know that the rulers of the Gentiles lord it over them, and their great ones exercise authority over them." Mt. 20:25

Sincerely in the Risen Lord,

Fr. Tom Heron

I refuse to let the Church be taken advantage of under the guise of "working together." Stewardship demands honesty, not low offers and unpaid rent.

His response, or lack thereof, reflected an entitlement that I found deeply troubling. He ignored invoices for months on end, despite repeated reminders. When pressed, he leaned on his connections to various superiors, who seemed more interested in placating the Fraternity than in supporting the canonical authority of a pastor. One monsignor, in particular, was relentless in his push for "Christian charity," urging me to accept the Fraternity's offer as a demonstration of goodwill. But this wasn't a matter of charity; it was a business transaction. Charity does not mean allowing oneself to be taken advantage of, especially when the financial health of a parish is at stake.

By 2020, after nearly two years of back-and-forth, the archbishop entered the scene. He was new to the archdiocese and inherited this tangled web of conflict. When I met with him in March of that year, he was refreshingly receptive. He understood the injustice that had been allowed to fester and assured me that the property would not be sold to the Fraternity. It was a moment of relief, though the scars of the battle remained. My "opponent's" tactics had not only been unethical but had also drained valuable time and energy that could have been devoted to pastoral work.

January 3, 2020

Reverend J. Thomas Heron

Dear Father Heron,

Best wishes for a Happy New Year. May 2020 be filled with God's blessings.

In December, gave me the surprising news that rejected the Letter of Intent submitted to you by on behalf of the parishioners of the When we met with on October 14 of last year, all parties were in agreement that the best solution was for the parishioners of to purchase that property at a fair price. It seems that a difference in the understanding of what a "fair price" actually would be is at the heart of your parish's rejection of the Letter of Intent.

I write now to ask you and your Parish Councils to reconsider the offer from the parishioners of . This request comes not just from me, but also from who wants to accept the offer from the parishioners of The reasons we are encouraging your parish to accept the offer are based both on Christian charity and on basic practicality.

Christian charity calls us to help and support our fellow Catholics whenever we can. This is one such opportunity for the parishioners of to help and support fellow believers working to establish a different sort of Catholic parish. Disagreeing with the approach they take does not negate our obligation to help each other. Helping support other Catholics also demands that we not use them in any way to make an unreasonable profit from them.

On a practical level, the offer that parishioners have made is the best possible offer will receive for the property. Appraised values based on best possible use will never be realized since circumstances have shown that the Archbishop cannot relegate the Church. Parishioners of the former have indicated they will appeal any relegation. is certain that any appeal will be upheld by Rome, and so Church cannot be relegated for the foreseeable future. Accepting the offer of the present parishioners of is the only viable option now for Parish to consider.

Reverend J. Thomas Heron
January 3, 2020
Page 2

Please share this letter with members of your Parish Finance Council and Parish Pastoral Council. It is important that everyone involved in moving toward a decision on this proposed sale knows that and Archdiocesan administrators are asking and its parishioners to accept the offer for and rectory presented in the Letter of Intent submitted by Christian fellowship and charity toward the parishioners of call for acceptance. It also provides a measure of justice and fairness to the parishioners of who have worked hard to strengthen their parish.

I am happy to meet with you and either separately or jointly to discuss this request. It is vital to help both parish communities move forward.

With best wishes, I am

Sincerely in Christ,

When I heard this plea from Archdiocesan leadership, it felt more like a veiled directive than a request … a wolf in sheep's clothing.

What made this situation all the more disheartening was the broader context of parish mergers and property sales. Over the years, I had successfully navigated the sale of other properties. These were not easy tasks, but they were handled with integrity and a commitment to fairness. In each case, I ensured that the proceeds benefitted the parishioners who had sacrificed so much to keep their communities alive. To see that same commitment undermined by manipulative tactics was infuriating.

The priest's behavior reached its nadir when he openly admitted that he had been advised by the monsignor to ignore my invoices. This blatant disregard for ecclesiastical protocol and basic decency was a stark reminder of the challenges pastors face when navigating the intersection of ministry and business. It wasn't just about money; it was about respect, justice, and the preservation of trust within the Church.

In one of my final letters to the archbishop, I enclosed copies of all the invoices that had been ignored, along with documentation of the Fraternity's failure to uphold their financial obligations. I quoted Horace: "To flee vice is the beginning of virtue."[23] The vice in this case was not only the Fraternity's neglect but also the diocesan leadership's initial complicity in enabling such behavior. It was a systemic issue, one that required not only pastoral firmness but also a willingness to confront uncomfortable truths.

July 30, 2020

I am enclosing a copy of all the invoices I sent to He consistently ignored each one.

I told after I met with you on March 24, 2020, that the sale of the property to the Fraternity is on hold. I communicated this message to again when we met with on June 17th. Enclosed is a copy of Church bulletin dated June 28, 2020.

How long, O Lord!

***"To flee vice is the beginning of virtue."* ~ Horace**

In Corde Christi,

Fr. Tom Heron

Despite months of ignored invoices and fruitless meetings, I made it crystal clear: The sale was on hold. But delays without accountability breed frustration. How long, O Lord?

I am reminded of the wisdom of my grandfather, who often said, "Be gentle as a dove and sly as a fox." This balance of humility and shrewdness was essential in navigating this debacle. It was a lesson in standing firm without losing sight of the Gospel values that guide our actions. The seminary may not prepare you for battles like these, but life as a pastor demands a resilience that can only be forged in the crucible of experience.

In the end, the property was not sold to the Fraternity, and justice prevailed. But the journey to that outcome was a sobering reminder of the complexities of parish leadership. It is a role that requires not only spiritual wisdom but also the courage to confront challenges head-on, even when the odds seem stacked against you.

THE DAYS OF 'FATHER KNOWS BEST' ARE BEHIND US

This chapter is living proof that priests, like the communities they serve, navigate a world fraught with tension, disagreement, and competing priorities. But even conflict holds within it the seeds of grace. The Good Shepherd disputes and the debacle in Conshohocken reveal the deeply human dynamics at play within faith communities; dynamics shaped by pride, fear, misunderstanding, and, at times, a profound resistance to change.

Yet, the Gospel reminds us that conflict is nothing new. Jesus, in His earthly ministry, modeled the perfect balance between truth and love when faced with conflict. He famously called out the injustices of the Pharisees in the temple when he said, "Is it not written: 'My house shall be called a house of prayer for all peoples'? But you have made it a den of thieves." (Mark 11:17). He further denounced them for their hypocrisy. "You cleanse the outside of cup and dish, but inside they are full of plunder and self-indulgence. Blind Pharisee, cleanse first the inside of the cup, so that the outside also may be clean." (Matthew 23:25-26).

Even His disciples were not immune to His sharp tongue, which was rooted in wisdom and truth. "Why are you terrified, O you of little faith?" (Matthew 8:26); and, "Get behind me, Satan. You are thinking not as God does, but as human beings do." (Mark 8:33).

Jesus's approach was flush with integrity and compassion. He engaged with others not to dominate but to illuminate. His words, though firm at times, were always spoken with the aim of conversion and healing. And even in the face of betrayal, Jesus chose to extend grace. This chapter reminds us that to follow His example means to confront tension not with fear or aggression but with a heart anchored in Gospel truth.

Let us move from the trenches of conflict to the sanctuary of spiritual direction, where we encounter the undeniable truth that even the shepherd needs guidance. In moments of tension and uncertainty, receiving the wisdom of a spiritual director can illuminate paths that seem otherwise obscured. For me, such relationships became lifelines, offering clarity, fortitude, and a reminder that even in the darkest valleys, God provides the light of wisdom through His instruments.

CHAPTER 6

A Soul's Compass

THE GIFT OF SPIRITUAL DIRECTION

In every priest's journey, there are voices that resonate beyond the cacophony of daily life that cut through uncertainty and provide clarity, wisdom, and a reminder of one's calling. For me, that voice was Monsignor Dan Murray. My spiritual director, mentor, and cherished friend, Dan was the steady compass that guided my early years in seminary and continued to influence my priesthood long after I left its cloistered halls. His presence in my life was nothing short of providential, and his impact remains etched in my soul.

Our first meeting was unremarkable in its simplicity, yet it marked the beginning of one of the most significant relationships of my life. It was my second day in the seminary, where I found myself in the gym, shooting hoops to pass the time. Dan was there too, casually sinking shots, his demeanor as unassuming as his simple priestly collar. We struck up a conversation—ordinary enough—but it wasn't long before our discussions would take on a depth that would shape my vocation. Soon, I began meeting with him for spiritual direction, an arrangement that would last until his death on June 26, 2014. Over those years, our conversations became lifelines; spaces of challenge, growth, and spiritual revelation.

Dan had a way of seeing through you, of cutting past superficialities to the heart of the matter. His piercing insight could be intimidating, but it was always tempered by a genuine desire to help you become the person God intended you to be. He was direct, almost brusque at times, but never unkind. For Dan, spiritual direction was not a casual exercise; it was a sacred commitment, one that required honesty, vulnerability, and a willingness to be stretched beyond your comfort zone. If you weren't serious about growing in your spiritual life, Dan had little patience and time for you.

"Are you serious about doing this?" he'd ask with that probing look of his. "Because if you're not, find someone else. I'm not going to waste time."

Our sessions were rarely brief. Monthly meetings would easily stretch to two hours, with Dan pressing me to dive deeper into questions I thought I'd already answered. He'd hand me an index card at the end of each session, scrawled with two or three pointed questions for me to reflect on before our next meeting—questions like, "What is your vision of life?"; "What is your understanding of the Blessed Trinity?"; "Do you have a reflective approach to living?"; "How do you pray?"; "Do you possess a reverential approach to all of creation?"; and, "Do you expect to discover Divine love daily? Where?"

Tom,

Two very good articles.
We must speak of them sometime

Yours in Jeremiah 31:3

Tom, Two very good articles. We must speak of them sometime. Yours in Jeremiah 31:3

They weren't easy questions. He was a keenly observant man. His talent for noticing became the cornerstone of his approach to the spiritual life, along with his understanding of Sacred Scripture and thought, influenced by Bernard Lonergan.

I am reminded of St. Ignatius Loyola's wisdom, "We should not fix our desires on health or sickness, wealth or poverty, success or failure, a long life or a short one. For everything has a potential of calling forth in us a deeper response to our life in [the Blessed Trinity, Father, Son, and Holy Spirit.]"[24]

Dan's aim was never to affirm the answers I'd already arrived at but to expand my horizons, to challenge the narrow perspective of an eighteen-year-old seminarian, and to awaken in me a deeper self-awareness. "The spiritual life," he'd often remind me, "is never in isolation. It's always tied to what makes you a whole human being: the physical, intellectual, emotional, social, and spiritual dimensions of life. You can't separate them if you want healthy spiritual growth."

It's hard to overstate how formative those sessions were. Dan didn't just shape my understanding of Scripture and theology, though his expertise in those areas was unparalleled, he shaped my understanding of myself. He had this uncanny ability to identify the blind spots in my thinking and to draw out truths I hadn't yet seen. And he never let me off easy. When I'd offer a simplistic or surface-level answer, he'd press me.

"Is that really the best you can do? Rethink it and come back with something better."

Far from frustrating, his persistence inspired me. I wanted to rise to the standard he set because I knew it wasn't just for him, but it was for me, for the people I would one day serve, and ultimately for God.

One could guarantee that when engaged with Dan Murray, you were going to get the most direct communication. It could sometimes be interpreted as harsh or brash. He didn't mince words.

Yet, he had a gift for writing that was as sharp and purposeful as his spoken words. Over the years, he wrote me numerous letters, each one meticulously composed and overflowing with insight. Some were brief, offering a reflection or a question to consider. Others stretched to three or four pages, canvassing the spiritual, theological, or even practical challenges I was facing at the time.

May 14, 1977

Dear Tom,

Here are some random thoughts of an interested bystander. All people are in search of meaning. When that search is for a living word and they meet with a man in whose life everyone's inner preoccupations have gained, as it were, a tactile and visible form, then their interest is immediately awakened and the message finds a willing audience. People will find in you such a man. Take care of the gift.

Throughout your life it has been your great goof fortune to have your heart touched with fire. The fire of parents' love and care, the fire of the Spirit in Baptism, Confirmation, and tomorrow, Father and Son will love you and touch you with a profound Spirit-fire-love that will be with you every day of your life. I mention too my love that has touched you in its own way. Take care of the gift.

There is nothing more astonishing than life, just as it is; nothing more miraculous than growth and change and development. And as happens so often when we stop to regard God's work there is nothing to do but wonder and thank him, realizing how little we planned, how little we achieved and yet how much has been done. Be thankful and care for the gift.

The ultimate measure of a man is not where he stands in moments of comfort and convenience but where he stands at times of challenge and controversy. The true deacon-servant will risk his position, his prestige, and even his life for the welfare of others. In dangerous valleys and hazardous pathways he will lift some bruised and beaten brother to a higher and more noble life. Be a deacon, Tom. Take care of the gift.

Have we not learned that life is a profound and passionate love-affair? When you lie prostrate tomorrow you will experience the deep humanity of God. You will hear his whisper that says I understand your weakness, your confusion, your doubts. You will hear him say how sympathetic he is to all the painful struggle in which you will be engaged on his behalf. You will hear him graciously offer his strength and his help. And as you stand up again you will rest quietly secure in your closeness to him reassured that you will always be treated with infinite tenderness. Take care of the gift.

At tomorrow's ceremony we will be at the roots of reverence and respect. The action will be centered in the other and others according to their beauty, truth, goodness, and promise—especially promise of God man and world as gift. We are gift to each other. We are received from another. We are a gift that is given. We are grace. Take care of the gift.

This letter, given to me the day before my diaconate ordination, has lived in my heart ever since...

Tomorrow will be a day of surprise, of awe, of amazement, a day of wonder—the wonder we feel before the simplest flower; the wonder we feel at the touch of the hand of a friend, of God himself. Tomorrow will be a day of knowledge and intimacy. Knowledge will beget mystery; intimacy begets awe and the holy. Tomorrow will be like coming home. Appreciate the gift.

Scripture reminds us that we will be led by a child. Children instruct us fundamentally and movingly. They warm us against the death of wonder. The simplicity of the human heart is celebrated in the child's wide-eyed rush to the light, to the flower, to whatever is new. There is a thunderous noise in the smile of a child. The eyes grow big, the hands reach out, stop reverently; their touch is chaste; there is delight, total involvement and not a shred of self. We are to be as children, all of us. Treasure the gift.

The lesson of tomorrow is clear: friendship is grace. It takes a man alive with the fidelity of God to see really, to love wholly his fellow man in all his need. Beauty becomes wonder becomes being born again.

My gift is my love, symbolized in two flowers, green, growing, vibrant, alive. They are tiny and in need of much care. Learn what they need to live. Tom, take care of the gift.

Dan

...a reminder that all is gift, and that our truest calling is to become a gift for others.

Two of his letters stand out in particular: one written before my ordination as a deacon, and the other before my ordination as a priest. In both, Dan managed to capture the gravity of the moment while simultaneously reminding me of the joy and privilege of the priesthood. Those letters are treasures I still keep close, their wisdom as relevant today as it was then.

I often marveled at Dan's ability to express so much with so few words. His writing style, like his personality, was precise and unembellished. He had no patience for verbosity or flowery language. Instead, he wrote with clarity and purpose, distilling complex ideas into simple truths. As the head of the Scripture department at the seminary, he brought that same clarity to his teaching, challenging his students to engage with the Word of God in a way that was both intellectually rigorous and deeply personal. He once joked that he had read every book that lined the walls of his office, a claim I found dubious given the sheer number of them. Still, his depth of knowledge was undeniable, and I soaked up every opportunity to learn from him.

But Dan wasn't just a scholar or a spiritual director; he was a man of unlimited integrity and humility. I'll never forget an early encounter that revealed just how much I had to learn about those virtues. It was during a basketball game between the seminary's upper and lower divisions, a spirited rivalry that brought out my competitive streak. I had scored 36 points in the game, and Father Charlie O'Rourke, the spiritual director for the lower division, made a point of mentioning my performance to Dan the next day.

I couldn't resist correcting him: "It wasn't 30 points, Father, it was 36."

Dan stopped in his tracks, looked at me with a mixture of amusement and reproach, and said, "Who does this kid think he is?"

It was a moment that stuck with me, a gentle but pointed reminder of the importance of humility, a virtue Dan modeled effortlessly.

Dan's mentorship extended far beyond the seminary years. As I transitioned into the priesthood, hc remained a constant presence, offering guidance and encouragement through letters and phone calls. His reflections on Scripture, often shared in his diocesan-wide publications, were a source of inspiration not just for me but for countless other priests and deacons. He had a unique ability to bring the Word of God to life, to make it relevant and accessible without ever watering it down. His reflections were always rooted in the realities of human experience, yet they never lost sight of the divine.

The letters that follow are more than words on a page; they are sacred echoes of a friendship rooted in faith, a testament to the transformative power of spiritual direction. It is my hope that as you read them, you too will be inspired to seek out the voices in your life that draw you closer to the heart of the Blessed Trinity. For in those voices, as Dan so often reminded me, lies the compass that can guide us through the storms of life and into the peace of His presence.

PAY ATTENTION TO YOUR SOUL INSTEAD

1972 –

MADONNA AND CHILD
BY CONCHA MARIA GUTIERREZ NAVAS

May the Peace and Happiness
of Christmas
Be Yours Today and Every Day
Throughout the Coming Year

Dear Tom, "We know that the Father makes all things work together for the good of those who love Him and have been called according to His purpose." This is Paul's resounding manifesto of belief in the faithfulness of a loving God. It must be yours also. To make it a part of you—to eat these words so that they put flesh on your bones—you must be gentle with yourself and try to be present to all those things you've ever kept warm in your loving heart. You must try to remember the moments when you felt clearly the gift of being truly alive. This is what peace and integrity are all about. If you live in these you grow in the wonder of His love, as I've said to you before. He continually gives Himself to you, even in your "down days," in the midst of frustration and impatience. Integrity, justice, and tenderness characterize His way with you and mark the light which illumines your way within yourself. Sleep secure in His peace. Faithfulness has always been the hallmark of His love for you. It must be the measure of your joy in hope. Never give up on Him, never give up on you. Joy is He within your coming home. He loves you — so do I.

Dan's Christmas card from 1972 remains among the earliest tangible reminders of his ability to frame ordinary experiences with extraordinary insight. At the time, I was just beginning to find my footing in the seminary, navigating the uncharted waters of discernment while dealing with the quiet suspicions of fellow seminarians. Many of them misinterpreted my ease with faculty as a calculated attempt to curry favor. In reality, I was simply being myself: a young man curious and eager to learn. Dan understood this. He saw through the insecurities of others and urged me to stay grounded. His words reflected his understanding of human frailty, his warning against inordinate expectations during the Christmas season resonating not just in the moment but for years afterward.

"You can't will yourself into joy," he would remind me. "Pay attention to your soul instead."

Dan would say, too, that most people get depressed around Christmastime because they have inordinate expectations that Christmas is only supposed to be a time of joy and happiness. He would say, no, you can't predict when your down days are going to come and what causes them, but you have to be attentive to that. Come Hell or high water, I'm going to be happy. You can't bang your fists on the table and will it to be. It doesn't work that way.

Christmas, 1973

Dear Tom,

The power of Scripture is on my mind these days. It speaks to me and to you. I'd like to share some of that Word with you and speak to you, as always, heart to heart.

The book of Wisdom speaks first:
"When peaceful silence enveloped everything and night had run the half of her swift course, your all-powerful Word leaped from heaven's royal throne. Into the heart of a doomed land the stern warrior leaped." I always pause at the words "peaceful silence", "night running her swift course", and at the idea of God's word "leaping from heaven." What powerful images! This Word leaps into hearts. This Word speaks of God's love for you, for me. This Word cannot wait to leave heaven to tell you who you are; to tell you how God dreams—of you; to tell you that you are the apple of your Father's eye.

The prophet Isaiah speaks of the mystery of God in a child:
"A child is born to us, a son is given us; upon his shoulder dominion rests. They name him Wonder-Counselor, God-Hero, Father-Forever, Prince of Peace. His dominion is vast and forever peaceful. Then the wolf shall be a guest of the lamb and the leopard shall lie down with the kid. The calf and the young lion shall browse together with a little child to guide them… The baby shall play by the cobra's den and the child lay his hand on the adder's lair. There shall be no harm in all my holy mountain; for the earth shall be filled with Knowledge of the Lord as water covers the sea."

This has always been a text that causes me to pause. Like Elijah, we oftentimes fail to look for God in the gentle whisper of a breeze; who would think of finding the power of God in a child? Yet the obvious must never be forgotten and certainly Christmas is the night of the obvious, of the simple, of the profound. This child became a man; he came with an open heart, giving himself, calling you to be what you were created to be. He comes to you tonight where you are. He wants to show you the mountain tops, the green of the valleys and give you a vision. "The night is gone," he says, "it's morning." We do believe his eyes, Tom, because we see with the heart.

I'd leave you with these final thoughts:
All those who love you have given you the means of growing spiritually just because they love you; they have brought out in you the being that you would never have dared to become alone—that you never would have let yourself be.

Christmas is a time for remembering.
I remember a young boy of four years ago—running.
I remember his enthusiasm in speaking of his first love—his mother, his father, his family.
I remember "hearing him smile" so often as he very poet-like shared his dreams, his fears, his joys.

Even in my earliest years as a priest, it was letters like this—from those who saw something in me I could not yet name—that became steppingstones to grace…

I remember the day this summer when he became to me—in a special, actual way—a son.
I remember too the day he became a man—crossing that chasm and how his eyes spoke more of his joy than even his words could.

Christmas is a time for thanking.
I thank God for you.
I thank God for letting me see Him in you.
I thank God and am deeply grateful to you for what you daily teach me about the issues and dignity of life.

Tom, sleep now that you may dream
    dream that you may wake
    wake that you may sing again the song:
    Be.

An appreciative
Father

...the gift of spiritual fatherhood, received before it was ever fully claimed, reminded me: we are called to be before we are called to do.

The following year's Christmas letter was even more poignant. Dan captured the transformative moments of my early formation with striking clarity, recounting my journey from a young seminarian stumbling over questions of identity to a man awakening to the grace that had always surrounded him. His ability to frame these memories as a gift—both to me and to those who loved me—left an indelible mark. "Grace builds on nature," he believed, teaching me to see the interplay of humanity and divinity not as opposing forces but as a beautiful partnership in the hands of the Father, Son, and Holy Spirit. His letters weren't just reflections; they were signposts, guiding me deeper into the mystery of God's love.

'74

Dear Tom,

I had to share this with you. We've talked, especially the last time, of God's love, and how he speaks to the heart, of how his words gush from his heart seeking entrance to your heart. I know you'll understand this as well as these two papers written by one of the nuns I teach on Friday's. I know you'll see what is being said. I hope you get a chance to steal away from the preoccupations of the day and find the quiet necessary to read not just with your eyes, but also with your heart.

The first paper, the longer one, is on priesthood. I had spoken with the nuns about Jesus and Jeremiah and what kind of men they must have been. Using that as a basis for their own reflections I asked them to write a talk they would give to prospective priests.

The second paper, is on Moses. We had discussed his role in leading Israel thru the desert and how we all need a Moses to lead us and how many would like to play that role. She (the nun) wrote this on her own.

P.S. You should write.
P.S.S. I never think of you without thanking God.

Sincerely, with love,
Moses

Dear Tom, I had to share this with you, as we talked, especially the last time, of God's love, and how he speaks to the heart, of how his words gush from his heart seeking entrance to your heart. I know you'll understand this as well as these two papers written by one of the nuns I teach on Fridays. I know you'll see what is being said. I hope you get a chance to steal away from the preoccupations of the day and find the quiet necessary to read not just with your eyes, but also with your heart. The first paper, the longer one, is on priesthood. I had spoken with the nuns about Jesus and Jeremiah, and what kind of men they must have been. Using that as a basis for their own reflections, I asked them to write a talk they would give to prospective priests. The second paper is on Moses. We had discussed his role in leading Israel through the desert and how we all need a Moses, to lead us and how many would like to play that role. She (the nun) wrote this on her own. P.S. You should write. P.P.S. I never think of you without thanking God. Sincerely, with love, Moses

In a letter to me in 1974, Dan shared insights from his teaching, coupling his academic acumen with his deep understanding of pastoral care. He had a gift for grounding the theoretical in the real, urging me to imagine myself ministering to families in the throes of unimaginable grief—a child lost to a car accident, a young life stolen too soon. "Don't give them platitudes," he wrote. "Be present. Be real. That's what they need." It was advice I would carry with me into countless homes and hospital rooms, often finding that silence and presence spoke volumes when words felt insufficient.

Dan's humanity was always tempered by grace, and his encouragement to see divine love reflected in human encounters taught me to minister not from a place of answers but of shared vulnerability. He ends it with that subtle hint of humor he often had, penning his signature as "Moses." What I still find remarkably hilarious is that Dan never got a joke. But here, he's the jokester!

VOCATIONAL INFLUENCE

June 6, 1978

Dear Tom,

When the first preachers of the Gospel went on their first assignment they were given instructions by one who loved them as He was loved by his Father.
He told them—"The gift you have received, give as a gift."
Be the body of my Son, says the Father. Be open, be permeable, be needy, be at rest, be on the Way, be beset with suffering, be growing, be becoming, be contemplative, be creative, be unique, be generated.

Jesus prayed for them before he died. He prayed they would stay close to him, have a sense of direction, an intensity of life surrounding them. Be a man of faith-mystery that is destined to incarnate itself or die.

Be neither rebel nor idle servant, a writer once said. Rather constantly explore and enlarge the known frontiers of the Kingdom, the visible geography of the Spirit.

"I am sending you as lambs among wolves" he said. A most intriguing statement. An honest warning. You are the lamb, Tom. It is hard to imagine a more helpless creature than a lamb—so young, so vulnerable, so quiet, so peaceful, so spotless, so great a victim for reconciliation and forgiveness. But who are the wolves? This is where another statement of His comes in: "Be sly as a fox and gentle as a dove." Some versions say: "You must be clever as snakes and innocent as doves. The wolf in mythology and in reality comes in many disguises. Be on your guard—it is your worried Father who speaks. You will experience fiery ordeals; sometimes your inner harmony will be threatened; you will feel selfishness assert itself; routine can get you down; the contempt of others will discourage you. These are wolves.

No one had to tell Jesus about human nature. He knew men so well, all of them, that he needed no evidence from others about a ma for he himself could tell what was in a man. Men and women can be wolves too. "What do you seek?" is such a key question of the fourth Gospel. The hidden agenda problem we have so often spoken of. Never forget it. Jesus didn't because he remained whole and never forgot the love of his Father. The "men" Jesus knew included his disciples. For you "men" will be anyone who seeks you. If they do not seek the Lord through you then they are the hypocrite so often mentioned in the Gospels. "Don't cast your pearls to survive." Respect everyone, Tom, and be sure they see and respect the sacred in you.

In the midst of such a realistic missionary discourse by Jesus we hear in the background the consistent tone of freshness in His Good News. He encourages a virile resistance to evil, He constantly calls to a new age, and he promise new resources to meet new crises.

Dan Murray's call to be honest, to be holy, and to be on guard, without losing the wonder of the Gospel.

It was a period of monumental excitement and uncertainty, as I stepped into my first priestly assignment in 1978. His letter to me, rich with Scripture, urged me to be "as wise as serpents and as innocent as doves." He warned me of the wolves I would inevitably encounter, not to dissuade me but to help me stand firm in my identity as a priest. But what new priest wants to hear about wolves?! I thought I was going to go in and be the greatest thing since sliced bread. Yet, his words were humbling, reminding me that challenges were ahead, but the Blessed Trinity's hands would sustain me through them. That letter became my daily bread, a source of strength in the early, often tumultuous days of my ministry.

His ability to select different scripture passages and give a two-sentence commentary on how it would directly impact now my going to a parish as a priest is just remarkable. He could take life experience and scriptural passages and weave them in such a way that would enable me, even though I'm new to this role and experience, to try to be more attentive in this new experience.

The first unskippable step of the spiritual life is to be awake, be alert, be vigilant, be on guard. He wanted that for me. So, he gave me passages to read, such as Matthew 10, Marc 6, Luke 9, and expect me to reflect upon them. That's an extraordinary gift that the other nine seminarians I was ordained with did not have the privilege to receive.

Reference written by Monsignor Daniel A. Murray
Chairman, Scripture Department, Saint Charles Borromeo Seminary
1979

To: Princeton University, Center for Continuing Education

Dear Sir,

My association with J. Thomas Heron began nine years ago. In that time I have been his teacher, advisor, and guide.

He has many outstanding personal traits. The characteristic trait, however, that this man possesses, and which best sums up his personality, is integrity. Anyone who comes to know him soon becomes aware of the wholesomeness of his life.

He shows in academic matters a natural inquisitiveness and what some would call an "unrestricted desire to know." He has admirable discipline in his study habits and integrates his course of study into his personal life. Such discipline and integration enhance his ability to do research.

Princeton could not go wrong in admitting him to its program.

I recommend him without reservation.

Dan's words about integrity, discipline, and the desire to know have served as both encouragement and accountability throughout my life.

Perhaps the most extraordinary testament to Dan's faith in me came in the form of a reference letter he wrote in 1979, recommending me for a program at Princeton. His description of me as a man of integrity, with "an unrestricted desire to know," touched me deeply. Coming from a man whose own life was a testament to both qualities, it felt like a profound blessing.

Dan believed in the power of education to expand horizons, a belief he lived out in his own scholarship and teaching. He wanted me to see beyond the walls of the seminary, to engage with Scripture not just as text but as a living Word that shaped and transformed lives. Dan wanted his students to be familiar with development and change. You didn't have to be a scholar to achieve that. His letter of reference expanded my horizon into a deeper understanding that there are different styles of communicating the meaning of Sacred Scripture.

COMING FULL CIRCLE

May 24, 1996

His Eminence

Dear Cardinal

Please excuse this perhaps irregular and eleventh hour intervention regarding the situation of Father J. Thomas Heron. I am writing this on my own initiative, not at his request. For the past twenty-six years I have been his spiritual director. After his conversation with you yesterday he visited me. When he left I began to draft this letter in the hope that you might take my thoughts into consideration.

The seminary needs a priest like Father Heron. I know that during my six years as rector I never found a more dedicated, more prayerful priest. He makes a holy hour early each morning between 5:00 and 6:00 A.M. The seminarians admired his prayerfulness, his honesty, his integrity and often made it a point to tell me how much they appreciated the prayerful role model he was. What a great loss to the seminarians his transfer would be. They so desperately need priests like Father Heron in formation especially given the circumstances of the day. He is completely dedicated to this most important work of forming future priests and I am convinced he could spend the rest of his priesthood in this ministry.

As an aside, his assignment at the seminary also allowed him to take care of his 75-year-old mother who has had no one but him to care for her and support her both financially and emotionally. I know he agonizes over how he will be able to do this if he is transferred and I think that was a principal reason he asked for one more year at the seminary. He feels he needed that time to get her prepared.

If you think, however, that he should not remain at Saint Charles I would respectfully recommend that you consider giving him time off in order to refocus his own mind and get spiritually settled, should he request this. The news of his transfer caught him completely by surprise and the perception he has that he is being unfairly treated is deeply felt. Father Heron has a spiritual dignity, Your Eminence, and he really has a need right now to hold onto it.

With the promise of my daily prayers for you, I remain

Respectfully yours in Christ,

Daniel A. Murray

Rev. Msgr. Daniel A. Murray, S.T.L., S.S.L.

A quiet testimony that sometimes, the most powerful advocacy comes unrequested, born of genuine brotherhood and concern.

. . .

Even as the years wore on and Dan's health began to decline, his letters lost none of their power. In 1996, he penned a deeply personal appeal to Cardinal Bevilacqua, advocating for me to remain at the seminary amidst a controversial transfer. His awareness of both grace and evil, of the need to discern between them, was sharper than ever. He feared that my naivety would make me susceptible to manipulation, and his letter was both a defense of my priesthood and a lesson in the complexities of human motives.

He said that evil that is conscious and malicious is one thing, but when people don't even know that they are engaged in evil behavior or evil decision making, that force of evil is even more harmful. He challenged me to differentiate between malicious evil and unconscious evil.

November 29, 2012

Reverend Monsignor Daniel Murray

Dear Dan,

As you turn past the ¾ pole today, I remember with fondness and frustration climbing the Mountain to Room 417 with my copy of the New Testament in hand. I was determined to learn about Jesus, the Kingdom of God, and the Sermon on the Mount from you. ("Did you read all these books.") Each time I would visit, you would greet me graciously and tell me to put the New Testament down on the table saying, "we will get to it later."

Now some 40 + years later, much like the two disciples on the road to Emmaus (although we have traveled more than seven miles) I give you two gifts as a token of my gratitude for the countless lessons you have taught and continue to teach me about the New Testament—abundant life, love—human and divine, discipleship, conversion, κένωσις and πληρόω.

May our travels continue. And may you continue to "open my eyes" and "set my heart on fire."

Cor ad cor,

Marking decades of brotherhood and formation, I wrote this letter to Msgr. Dan Murray on his birthday, honoring the journey we shared through Scripture, discipleship, and the gift of spiritual friendship, a road still unfolding, heart to heart.

By 2012, our relationship had come full circle, some forty years after we first met. I wrote to Dan, reflecting on our first meeting and the countless lessons he had taught me. I thanked him for opening my eyes to the beauty and challenge of priestly life, for setting my heart on fire with a love for Scripture and ministry.

"Our travels continue," I wrote, borrowing from the road to Emmaus, where Jesus walked with His disciples, their hearts burning within them. In many ways, Dan had been my companion on that road, opening my eyes to the truth and wonder of the priesthood.

Dan Murray's voice remains alive through these memories, speaking wisdom, encouragement, and challenge into my life and ministry. His mentorship was a reflection of the divine presence of Father, Son, and Holy Spirit, a reminder that even the shepherd needs guidance.

WE WALK TOGETHER IN GOD'S LIGHT AND LOVE

Even as his health began to decline in his later years, Dan continued to pour himself into his ministry and his relationships. His letters became more reflective, tinged with the wisdom of someone who had lived deeply and loved fully. He wrote about the challenges and joys of the priesthood, the importance of remaining grounded in prayer, and the need to approach every moment with a spirit of gratitude.

In his final years, his words carried an added poignancy, as if he knew his time was drawing to a close and wanted to impart as much wisdom as he could before he left this world.

When Dan passed away, it was a loss that shook me to my core. He had been more than a mentor; he had been a spiritual father, a friend, and a model of what it means to live a life fully devoted to the Gospel. Yet, even in his absence, his presence remains. I hear his voice in the questions I ask myself during prayer, in the way I approach difficult conversations, and in the way I try to guide others on their spiritual journeys.

His lessons, his letters, and his example continue to shape me, reminding me that spiritual direction is not just about guidance, but about relationship, walking alongside someone as they seek to discover the depths of divine love.

The Gospel reminds us that Jesus Himself sought solitude with the Father but always returned to guide His disciples. He poured into them so that they, in turn, could pour into the world. Spiritual direction mirrors this sacred rhythm: receiving from Father, Son, and Holy Spirit, and trusted mentors so we might walk with others in their journey of faith. The words of Proverbs 27:17 ring true: "As iron sharpens iron, so one person sharpens another."[25] The lessons I received from Dan have shaped not only my ministry but also my call to accompany others in their spiritual growth.

We now move from the quiet, prayerful reflections of being guided to the active call of mentoring others. What does it mean to lead others closer to God? How can a priest become an instrument of grace for parishioners, friends, and even strangers? Let us now explore how the role of mentor emerges as an extension of discipleship and a response to Christ's invitation to "feed my sheep" (John 21:17).

CHAPTER 7

From Compass to Guide

BECOMING A MENTOR IN FAITH

The Gospel reminds us that no grace is given merely for our benefit alone. Jesus calls us to share freely the gifts we've received, to be conduits of His love and truth for others. St. Paul captures this sentiment so beautifully in his letter to the Corinthians.

> "Blessed be the God and Father of our Lord Jesus Christ, the Father of compassion and God of all encouragement, who encourages us in our every affliction, so that we may be able to encourage those who are in any affliction with the encouragement with which we ourselves are encouraged by God. (2 Corinthians 1:3-4)

I've often reflected on those words when considering how the gift of spiritual direction, first so generously bestowed upon me by Monsignor Dan Murray, became a gift I felt compelled to share with others. The wisdom, patience, and encouragement he poured into me were not meant to remain in me alone. They were seeds planted by the Blessed Trinity, seeds meant to take root and bear fruit in the lives of others.

Dan's guidance shaped me not just as a priest, but as a person. His questions taught me to pray more deeply, to see the movements of grace in the everyday moments of life. As I transitioned from being the mentee to becoming a mentor, I found myself often returning to the lessons he instilled in me that taught me how to listen with both the heart and the head, to lead with humility, and to walk alongside others as they sought the Lord's voice in their own lives. The shift felt natural, almost organic. I didn't set out to become a spiritual mentor. It began quietly, almost imperceptibly, when parishioners, students, and even colleagues began seeking my guidance.

In my earliest days of spiritual direction, I often found myself replicating Dan's approach. His method of offering questions or a single point for reflection was one I instinctively adopted. But, as I quickly learned, the gift of mentorship isn't about mimicking someone else's style, but discovering how to use your own gifts to meet the unique needs of the person sitting across from you. And, to be honest, my earliest efforts weren't always the most polished. I remember those days as a deacon at St. David's Parish. I was so eager, so enthusiastic. A parishioner would come to me for guidance, and I'd send them off with five books in hand, pages marked, eager for them to absorb everything I thought they needed to know in one sitting! Looking back now, I have to laugh at myself. I realize I was trying to fast-track their spiritual growth.

But, as I learned through experience—and some gentle corrections from my mentors—the spiritual life doesn't unfold on our timeline. Growth happens in its own season, much like a tomato ripens on the vine. You can't force it, nor should you try. People who want to really make progress in the spiritual life have a genuine, authentic hunger for it. You can't get discouraged when it's not immediately making sense. So, would you rather have a hot house tomato or one naturally grown? A hot house tomato is called that because it grows faster than the natural process. It's grown in a hot house and not in nature!

Everyone has their own spiritual rhythm. Whether they're aware of that or not is something to consider. You can make leaps in progress, but you can't force it. It's not a mechanical thing; it's a human progression. The first unskippable step of the spiritual life is to be attentive. You have to be attentive to what your particular rhythm is right now in making progress in the spiritual life. You can make, in a six-month period, a lot of progress, but then it may take another year and a half to make the same amount of progress because you're exploring something a little bit deeper in your personality that has either been neglected or buried or has been a deformative experience. It's going to take more to unravel a deformative experience and replace it with a healthier formative pattern. I often think of that image of the tomato, and I remind myself of it whenever I feel tempted to rush what only deep-rooted personal grace can accomplish.

One of my most vivid memories from those early years of spiritual mentorship was working with a husband and wife from St. David's Parish. They would come to me separately, seeking direction for their individual spiritual lives. Then, after a time, they decided to come together, asking for guidance as a couple. I remember feeling the weight of the challenge. How do you guide two individuals on their paths to holiness while helping them discover how their marriage is also a shared vocation of sanctification? Yet, in walking with them, I learned just how beautiful it is to see grace at work not only in individual souls but also in the sacred union of marriage. It was a humbling experience, and one that reminded me of the profound responsibility and privilege of this ministry.

There were others, too. A permanent deacon, early in his own ministry, came seeking direction. I recall being struck by his humility, his willingness to ask for help, even as he was preparing to serve others in his diaconate.

And there was a high school junior, a young woman on the cusp of adulthood, wrestling with the pressures of her age and searching for meaning. Sitting with her, I realized that spiritual direction isn't reserved for those of a certain age or maturity. The Spirit moves in every heart, regardless of how young or old it may be. Her questions reminded me of the deep thirst for God that resides in all of us, a thirst that so often begins to stir in unexpected ways during adolescence.

Of course, not everyone came intending to commit fully to spiritual direction. Some approached me more casually, hoping to gain wisdom without fully entering the process. They showed me that not everyone is in the same place on their journey, and that's okay. My role isn't to drag someone further along the path than they're ready to go. It's simply to meet them where they are, offering whatever encouragement and insight they're prepared to receive.

When I think about the people I've walked with over the years, I realize just how diverse their journeys have been. Some came seeking guidance during moments of crisis, others in times of quiet discernment. Some were young, like that high school girl; others were older, seasoned in life but still yearning to grow in their relationship with the Father, Son, and Holy Spirit. Each one was a reminder that the spiritual life is deeply personal, yet profoundly communal. We are all called to walk this path together, bearing one another's burdens and celebrating one another's joys.

I'm struck by the beauty of the call to mentor others in faith. It's not about having all the answers or being a perfect example. It's about being present, listening attentively, and pointing always toward Christ. The Gospel teaches us that Jesus walked with His disciples, teaching them not only through His words but through His very presence. He never stopped calling them to deeper faith. I strive to follow a model of spiritual mentorship rooted in love, humility, and a trust in the Holy Spirit's timing.

TENDING THE GARDEN OF GROWTH: CULTIVATING SOULS THROUGH PATIENCE

When I first met Sarah Bacza at St. Coleman's, she was navigating the challenges of young adulthood and discerning her path in the faith. At that time, she was working at the Newman Center at West Chester University, a spiritual hub for students seeking connection with the Catholic faith on a public campus. Our initial encounter occurred in the confessional, and soon after, she reached out to ask if I would become her spiritual director. I vividly remember her palpable hunger for spiritual growth.

Spiritual direction is a commitment, not a casual endeavor. When Sarah asked, I had to be upfront about my limited availability. I typically kept ten advisees at a time, and only when someone "bailed out" could I take on someone new. Her persistence and commitment were evident from the start, and I saw in her a genuine desire to grow. She began meeting with me every two weeks and later transitioned to every three weeks or monthly as our conversations deepened.

Sarah came to spiritual direction with a list of struggles she wanted to confront. Chief among them was her relationship with her parents. Like many young adults, she wrestled with the inevitable imperfections of family life. I recall telling her something that remains true for all of us: “There’s no perfect parent.” Parents, like all of us, carry both the wheat and the weeds of their humanity. It’s a truth rooted in the Gospel. St. Matthew reminds us that we must allow the wheat and weeds to grow together because their separation belongs to God’s timing, not ours. Sarah’s desire to "cleanse her life of weeds" was admirable but misguided. She needed to accept the presence of both—within herself and others—and to lean on grace to ensure the weeds did not dominate.

Her scrupulosity, however, often became a stumbling block. She sought perfection not only in her relationships but also in herself. At times, she would want me to make decisions for her, hoping I could relieve her of the burden of choice. But that is not the role of a spiritual director. Borrowing from Bernard Lonergan’s framework, I explained that I couldn’t change her life experiences; I could only help her understand them. I could guide her toward making reasonable judgments and meaningful decisions. I respected her too much to take ownership of her choices, no matter how young or inexperienced she might have felt.

Sarah needed time to distinguish what in her life was truly fruitful and what needed to be surrendered. It wasn't easy for her—fear and perfectionism clouded her vision—but through our sessions and the divine guidance of Father, Son, and Holy Spirit, she began to embrace this truth.

May 22, 2012

Dear Sarah,

All of us have deeply ambivalent feelings about change. What will never change is the desire to change and the fear of change. It is the desire to change that motivates us to seek counsel. It is the fear of change that motivates us to resist the very help we seek.

The desire to change and the desire to remain the same coexist for good reason. Both are essential to our emotional well-being and equally deserves our attention.

Our strengths and weaknesses are inseparable. Far from being opposites, they are woven from the same cloth of our personality.

Personal change will always be accompanied by inevitable frustration and setbacks. Someone once said, "In the spiritual journey you go three steps forward and two steps backward, but with perseverance you do finally achieve your (and the Blessed Trinity) destination—eternal life."

I believe you are embarking on the dark night of the senses and the dark night of the soul. Be assured of my daily prayers.

Sincerely in Our Lord,

Fr. Tom Heron

P.S. I thought and prayed about our meeting yesterday. The thoughts above are the fruit of my reflection. I hope they are helpful to you.

When offering counsel to a parishioner navigating spiritual struggle, I reflected on how the desire for change and the fear of change often live side by side in all of us.

In May 2012, I wrote Sarah a letter that reflected our ongoing conversations. I wanted to remind her of a crucial spiritual principle: change is both a desire and a fear. “The desire to change and the desire to remain the same coexist for good reason,” I told her. Both are woven into the fabric of our emotional well-being and deserve our attention. Sarah’s fear of change, though real, did not have the final word. Like all of us, she was a mixture of strengths and weaknesses, and her path forward required her to confront both with honesty and courage. As I concluded in the letter, "In the spiritual journey, you go three steps forward and two steps backward, but with perseverance, you achieve your destination—eternal life."

June 27, 2012

Dear Sarah,

Our meeting last night was intense. It will take time to absorb, assimilate, and appropriate all that was exchanged. Be gentle with yourself. Be patient. Intellectual conversion – Moral conversion – Spiritual conversion is a slow and often bloody process.

Know that new understanding, new freedom, and new peace awaits you.

Know also I shall clarify some important points that I left hanging.

Be assured of my prayers. Kindly pray for me and the people of St. Matthew Parish.

I go on vacation Sunday afternoon July 29th. I hope we can meet the week of July 23rd. Let me know.

"The meaning of life lies, not as we have grown used to thinking in prospering, but in the development of the soul." *Alexander Solzhenitsyn*

"No matter how deep our darkness, God is deeper still."

Sincerely in Our Lord,

Fr. Tom Heron

Real conversion, the kind that shapes eternity, demands patience, courage, and a heart willing to be broken open by grace.

Sarah's growth was steady but not without setbacks. By June, she had made significant progress, and I followed up with another letter to solidify what we had discussed. I encouraged her to take the time to absorb and reflect on her journey. Spiritual conversion, I reminded her, is a "slow and often bloody process." It cannot be rushed. Through intellectual, moral, and spiritual conversion, Sarah was discovering new freedoms, but she had to honor her rhythm of growth rather than force it. I asked her to pray, reflect, and engage deeply with the material we discussed, always seeking to internalize rather than merely parrot back what I shared with her.

What struck me most about Sarah was her determination. Despite her fears and proclivity toward perfection, she was willing to confront the complexities of her life with faith. She taught me, once again, the patience required in spiritual direction, both for the director and the directee. Each step forward, however small, was a testament to the presence of our Lord in her life.

My dear friend of 38 years, Mary Kay, whom I collaborated with in various apostolates, experienced a journey that was no less a testament to the power of faith to navigate life's upheavals. Mary Kay was a teacher, a mother, and a seeker. Her struggles were deeply intertwined with the competing demands of professional obligations, personal fears, and the daunting task of staying connected to her authentic self.

When her son Pierce was preparing to graduate from high school, it marked a significant shift in her life. With this transition came the weight of uncertainty. Mary Kay's fear often outweighed her faith, pulling her away from the stillness needed to discern her next steps. It was during this time that we explored two forms of prayer—spousal prayer and occupational prayer—as means to ground herself in God's presence.

Feb. 22, 2013

Dear Mary Kay,

Spousal love and the spiritual life is much more than living and working together. It is a bond of the heart and soul that has no physical limitations.

Jesus is the source of grace and peace in our hearts and in *all* of our relationships. It is vital to remind ourselves of this important truth from time to time.

1 When we feel stressed and overwhelmed, it is comforting to know Jesus is the source of grace and peace.

2 When we are hurt and rejected; when we are tired and unmotivated, Jesus is the source of grace and peace.

3 When we seem in control and responsible for our lives or anxious about all those things that did not go according to plan or get done Jesus is the source of grace and peace.

He is here with us, yet we long for him.
He feeds us, yet we hunger for him.
He heals us, yet we cry out for the medicine that only he can prescribe.
Our longing, our hunger, our cries for his healing love find their most profound expression in the surrender of ourselves, as Jesus gave himself for us. To give of ourselves in love is the grace and peace of Jesus Christ. Share my ritual with Pierce. Cor ad Cor – TOM

Dear Mary Kay, Spousal love and the spiritual life is much more than living and working together. It is a bond of the heart and soul that has no physical limitations. Jesus is the source of grace and peace in our hearts and in all of our relationships. It is vital to remind ourselves of this important truth from time to time. When we feel stressed and overwhelmed, it is comforting to know Jesus is the source of grace and peace. When we are hurt and rejected; when we are tired and unmotivated, Jesus is the source of grace and peace. When we seem in control and responsible for our lives or anxious about all those things that did not go according to plan or get done, Jesus is the source of grace and peace. He is here with us, yet we long for Him. He feeds us, yet we hunger for Him. He heals us, yet we cry out for the medicine that only He can provide. Our longing, our hunger, our cries for His healing love find their most profound expression in the moments of Eucharist—as Jesus gave Himself for us to give us salvation in love—in the grace and peace of Jesus Christ. Share my ritual with Pierce. *Cor ad cor* – Tom

Spousal prayer, as I explained to her, is the capacity to be fully present, absorbed in silence and solitude, allowing for a deeper union with God. Occupational prayer, by contrast, sanctifies the ordinary tasks of daily life, infusing them with purpose. "If you're cooking," I told her, "cook as if you're offering that meal to God. If you're sweeping the floor, sweep it with all the care and intention of creating something sacred." These practices are reminders to bring God into the rhythm of every moment, no matter how mundane.

Mary Kay often struggled with the gap between her experience and her expectations, particularly as a teacher, which was a calling she loved deeply but one that had become fraught with challenges. She wrestled with whether to remain in education or step away. We often discussed Bernard Lonergan's framework of meaning. The key in this situation, I reminded her, was attentiveness. By reflecting on her experiences, she could gain clarity about their deeper meaning, make reasonable judgments, and align her decisions with God's will.

3-10-03

Dear Mary Kay,

I am enclosing one excerpt from my journal – the Ash Wednesday entry

This Lent my prayer for you is that you will discover within a better way to handle fear (a utilitarian emotion). It seems to me that fear, whether it is real, imagined or anticipated causes you to see DANGER EVERYWHERE. That perception circles back and reinforces and increases your original fear. Wow, the fear is greater and the cycle is repeated rehearsed, replayed and unfortunately stubbornly held onto.

May you be attentive to this dynamic process in you. May you be receptive to the revelation by Jesus and the Holy Spirit that there is another option – a more humane way of responding to fear. May you discover that option – absorb it, assimilate it, appropriate it and BE CONVERTED by it.

We are all responsible (loaded word) for our own lives. Our behavior is a function of our decisions, not our circumstances and conditions.

Dear Mary Kay, I am enclosing one excerpt from my journal – the Ash Wednesday entry. This Lent my prayer for you is that you will discover within a better way to handle fear (a utilitarian emotion). It seems to me that fear, whether it is real, imagined or anticipated, causes you to see DANGER EVERYWHERE. That perception circles back and reinforces and increases your original fear. Wow, the fear is greater and the cycle is repeated, rehearsed, replayed and unfortunately stubbornly held onto. May you be attentive to this dynamic process in you. May you be receptive to the revelation by Jesus and the Holy Spirit that there is another option – a non-human way of responding to fear. May you discover that option – absorb it, assimilate it, appropriate it and BE CONVERTED by it. We are all responsible (loaded word) for our own lives. Our behavior is a function of our decisions, not our circumstances and conditions.

One letter I wrote to Mary Kay emphasized how fear can become an all-consuming force if left unchecked. It circles back and reinforces itself until it becomes a prison of our own making. Yet, fear and faith are not opposites but companions on the spiritual journey. I continued, "If we are frequently in repetitive manners of thinking, we often react rather than respond. Reactive mode quickly lead to fatigue and other negative worries." To move beyond the cycles of fear, I challenged her to embrace Longergan's philosophy: be attentive to your experience, be intelligent in understanding it, be reasonable in your judgments, and allow those judgments to guide meaningful decisions.

I encouraged her to reconnect with what I called her "core gifts" to be creative, playful, and simple. When we lose sight of these gifts, we risk living in chaos and fear. I urged her to recognize that fear does not have the final word. Faith invites us to see beyond fear, to embrace the creative possibilities that arise when we trust in God's guidance.

For Mary Kay, sometimes her struggle took the form of grief. Her ultimate call was to embrace her authentic self. Her journey required her to confront her deepest vulnerabilities. In doing so, she discovered what it means to truly rely on Father, Son, and Holy Spirit to live with her core values with conviction.

FAITH, MEMORY, AND LOVE: GUIDING HEARTS THROUGH TRANSITIONS

Grace Opiela was another individual whose journey in faith taught me intense lessons about the human heart's capacity to endure and grow. Our relationship began after a Sunday Mass, during which she shared her struggles with loss and the weight of life's uncertainties. Grace carried with her a "woe is me" disposition, often feeling overwhelmed by the challenges she faced. Yet beneath her burdens, I sensed a deep longing for hope and renewal.

Grace had recently experienced the loss of her husband, a man with whom she had shared every aspect of her life. Their marriage was one of deep companionship; they rarely spent time apart, and the void left by his absence was staggering for her. Yet as I listened to her, I realized that Grace's loss, while immense, was not an ending. It was a transformation.

January 2, 2013

Dear Grace,

St. Paul wrote to a fearful, persecuted Church in Rome, and apparently he fielded many questions about what was to happen, who would be handed over, who would be condemned, and how things would turn out in the end. He did not respond with explanations or predictions but with the confident voice of hope:

"Who will separate us from the love of Christ? Trial, or distress, or persecution, or hunger, or nakedness, or danger, or the sword? As Scripture says: "For your sake we are being slain all the day long; we are looked upon as sheep to be slaughtered." Yet in all this we are more than conquerors because of him who has loved us. For I am certain that neither death nor life, neither angels nor principalities, neither the present nor the future, nor powers, neither height nor depth nor any other creature, will be able to separate us from the love of God that comes to us in Christ Jesus, our Lord." Romans 8:35-39

Be assured of my continued prayers.

Sincerely in Our Lord,

Fr. Tom

Fr. Tom Heron

No trial, no fear, no force on earth can ever separate us from the love of Christ. When answers fall short, hope must rise.

I wrote her a letter shortly after our conversation, drawing from the words of St. Paul in Romans 8: "Who will separate us from the love of Christ? Trial, or distress, or persecution, or hunger, or nakedness, or danger, or the sword?" These words, written to a fearful and persecuted Church, echoed Grace's own fears. Like the Christians in Rome, she needed to be reminded that nothing—not even death—could separate her from the love of Christ or from the love she shared with her husband. Physical absence is a change, not an ending, I told her.

One of the most poignant moments in my correspondence with Grace came when I reflected on the transformative power of memory. I told her that memories, when shared, become living connections. They are not relics of the past but bridges to the present, allowing the deceased to remain with us in a way only explained by the presence of the Blessed Trinity. Grace embraced this idea, finding solace in recounting stories of her husband and hearing others share their own memories of him. It was a small but powerful step toward healing.

Grace's faith was deeply devotional, often rooted in prayers rather than Scripture. I respected this but sought to gently guide her toward the Good News as a source of strength and renewal. On one occasion, the liturgical reading for morning prayer was the very passage from Romans that I had shared with her. I saw it as a providential moment, a reminder that God's Word has a way of meeting us exactly where we are. I encouraged her to lean into these moments, to allow Scripture to speak into her grief and guide her forward.

Frank Corace was yet another example of how faith, memory, and love can heal the heart from loss. He and I shared a bond rooted in our shared experiences at Monsignor Bonner High School, where our mutual love for basketball forged an early connection. Though Frank graduated a decade before me, his reputation as an exceptional athlete preceded him. Frank's life on the court was nothing short of inspiring, but it was his journey through grief that revealed the quiet strength of his faith.

When Jovita, his wife, passed away, Frank faced the void left by her physical absence. I was honored to preside at her funeral, which drew a small, intimate group of mourners. As I prepared for the homily, I reflected on a question that arises in the wake of every loss: How do we sustain the bond with someone we love when death has altered the way we experience them?

The answer, as I often say, lies in faith, memory, and love. Faith assures us that death is not the end but a passage into new life. As I shared with Frank and those gathered, memory plays a vital role in bridging the physical absence. I encouraged them to recall Jovita in all her fullness: her smile, her laughter, her unique mannerisms. Memories, when shared, transform from isolated moments into living connections. The stories we recount bring the deceased into our present in a way that keeps them alive in our hearts and communities.

During the eulogy, I spoke of the Paschal Mystery—birth, life, suffering, death, and new life—and how this sacred rhythm is woven into our human experience. Faith doesn't demand immediate answers; it calls us to trust that God's love will sustain us through the mystery of grief.

March 8, 2022

Dear Frank,

Be assured of my prayers for the happy repose of your wife Jovita's soul and for you during these days of grief and loss. May your faith in the Risen Lord be a source of strength and comfort to you.

May memory and love heal Jovita's felt absence physically and connect you with her real presence spiritually.

"Weeping is the eloquence of sorrow. It is an unstammering orator, needing no interpreter, but understood by all. Tears are to be understood even when words fail! We need to learn that tears are liquid prayers of intercession which will wear its waý right into the very heart of mercy, despite the stony difficulties which obstruct the way."

Death is not some kind of unfortunate accident, but a reality sewn into the fabric of our faith—the Paschal mystery—birth, life, suffering, death, new life.

There is a thread that connects heaven and earth. If we find that thread everything is meaningful, even death. If we do not find that thread, that connection, nothing is meaningful, even life.

"The death of someone we love has a way of focusing the mind, heart, and soul."

"Remember, death ends a life, but not a relationship."

"What we once enjoyed and deeply loved we can never lose, for all that we love deeply becomes a part of us."

Sincerely in the Risen Lord,

Fr. Tom Heron

Guiding someone through the shadows of grief is one of the most sacred responsibilities of a priest. In this letter, I offered Frank not answers, but accompaniment … a spiritual hand to hold as he walks the valley of loss, reminding him that love, transformed by faith, does not end.

In a letter to Frank, I wrote: "Weeping is the eloquence of sorrow. It is an unstammering orator, needing no interpreter, but understood by all." Tears, I reminded him, are prayers of intercession, unspoken but deeply heard by the heart of God.

What I'm trying to impart in this message is that most people understand death as a tragedy, an accident, or an ending. From a faith perspective, death is woven right into the fabric of living. Sometimes it might take three years before an individual integrates a person's death into that fabric. It doesn't happen because you said it and at the snap of a finger you are at peace. Some people cling to being inconsolable. They'll dive onto the coffin as it's being lowered down. They might scream just to display their grief.

It was essential for Frank to allow himself to grieve, to lean into the pain without losing sight of the eternal connection he shares with Jovita. Like Grace, his relationship with his spouse had changed, but it had not ended. Faith, memory, and love continue to sustain that bond.

3/14/22

FROM THE DESK OF

Frank C. Corace

Tom

My personal thanks for your kind letter and inspirational messages. It means a lot to me with Jovita's passing. We had 56 good years together even though the last several had its good and trying moments.

She didn't suffer and the Dear Lord was good in taking her home early. We all will certainly miss her but knowing you and other good friends are praying for her is really comforting. Stay well good friend!!

Frank C.

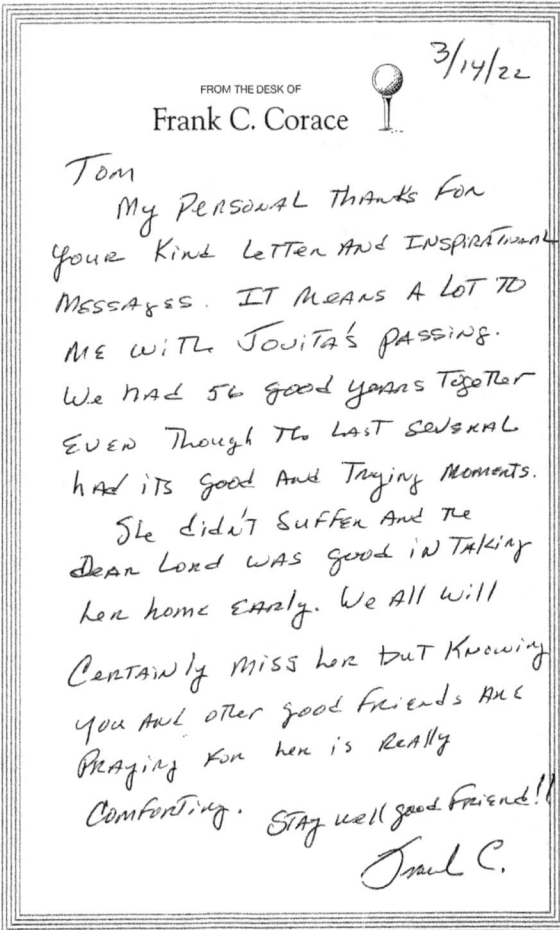

Tom, My personal thanks for your kind letter and inspirational messages. It means a lot to me with Jovita's passing. We had 56 good years together even though the last several had its good and trying moments. She didn't suffer and the Dear Lord was good in taking her home early. We all will certainly miss her but knowing you and other good friends are praying for her is really comforting. Stay well good friend!! Frank C.

ANCHORING RELATIONSHIPS IN THE ETERNAL

Marriage is a sacrament that mirrors the union of Christ and His Church, a relationship built on self-giving love and mutual surrender. Connor and Kate Dwyer sought to honor this sacred bond as they celebrated their first anniversary.

In the age of texting and social media, a note or a letter communicates more depth to an occasion like a wedding anniversary than a phone call, text, or even a greeting card you buy in the store. I would always want to reach or stretch myself and offer a newly married couple a little bit more than the standard or normal mode of communication. I like the idea of bringing my own bias to it.

Because of a hectic, busy lifestyle, I think we need something like a letter to put a pause on the monotony of life and at least give us an opportunity to reflect a little bit more deeply on life. Experience on top of experience on top of further experience without any reflection is more dehumanizing than it is humanizing. People feel that. they're running here and rushing there. They forget to step back. That's what the word retreat means: to step away from all of your experience and look at what's going on and see what can be done to make improvements to humanize it, that it be more enriching rather than draining.

December 31, 2012

Dear Connor and Kate,

A blessed and happy anniversary! I share with you a reflection that I read recently. "Those who wittingly or unwittingly make themselves the center of the universe are not happy, and everyone in their vicinity feels the unpleasant tug of their gravity. The one who talks incessantly about his or her accomplishments or woes, quickly becomes a bore and misses the opportunity for authentic relationships. Life is not all about 'me.' Marriage, if it a merger of egos—a merger of 'me's'—will fail. Ministry, if it about 'me,' is no longer ministry. The Lord's way draws us out of ourselves and teaches us the way of surrender to the other." Sober thoughts on your first anniversary.

Be assured of my prayers.

"Abraham Lincoln's ability to counter criticism with humor was legendary. When told that he was two-faced, he instantly responded, "If I had two faces, do you think I'd be wearing this face?"

Sincerely in Our Lord,

Fr. Tom Heron
Pastor

Marking their first year of marriage, I offered Connor and Kate a quiet word of spiritual direction and an invitation to deepen their understanding of the sacrament they share and to remain rooted in grace as they grow together.

In my note to them, I shared a reflection I'd recently encountered: "Marriage, if it is a merger of egos—a merger of 'me's'—will fail. Ministry, if it is about 'me,' is no longer ministry. The Lord's way draws us out of ourselves and teaches us the way of surrender to the other." These thoughts, though sober, were a reminder of the joy and grace found in surrendering our will to God and each other. Connor and Kate's love for one another was evident, but like all couples, they needed to be reminded that marriage is not just a union of two individuals but a partnership anchored in the all-knowing love of the Blessed Trinity.

INSPIRATION IN REFLECTION AND ARTICULATION OF THE TRUTH

As children of God and students of Jesus Christ, we all navigate the uncertainties of change, grief, and discernment. Gifts such as faith, memory, and love invite us to pause and reflect, to trust in the Holy Spirit's timing, and to hold fast to the relationships that shape and sustain us.

Growth in the spiritual life demands patience, humility, and a willingness to embrace the tension between fear and faith, between what is and what could be.

A shining example is Angelina Heyse. I met her not long after she started attending St. Matthew's. She was a recent college graduate at the time and facing much uncertainty in life. She was not only struggling with the potential harm the COVID-19 virus could cause to her future plans of marriage and starting a family, but also with her career, her mental health, and her spirituality.

Like many, she came to me for spiritual direction with her own expectations of how it would work. Yet, she was a fast and eager learner, wise beyond her years. She recently wrote a letter to me that places a beautiful bow on this topic.

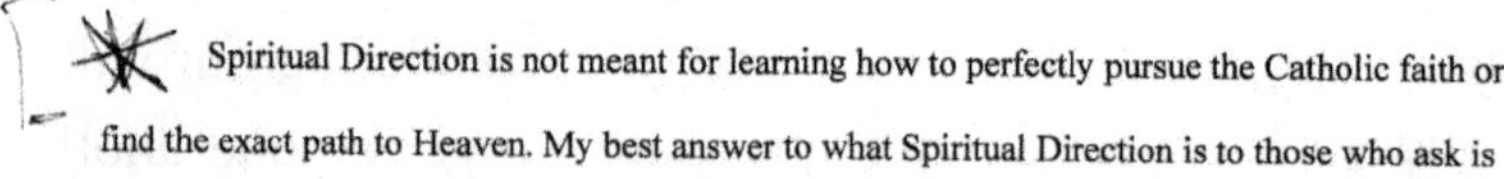
Spiritual Direction is not meant for learning how to perfectly pursue the Catholic faith or find the exact path to Heaven. My best answer to what Spiritual Direction is to those who ask is

it is a journey and a space to learn and ask questions. As we walk through life we are going to be faced with many challenges, successes, failures, and most importantly choices. We are not meant to know the answer to every question and not every choice we make will be the right one, but having a guide who can teach us to discern and pursue true holiness as well as wholeness is a gift. We are body and soul and our souls need guidance towards the Lord in the world we live today. I often pray that everyone continue to wonder and ask questions instead of getting stuck in accepting the answers and lies we are fed and bombarded with each and every day for someone else's personal gain.

I also pray everyone be gifted a spiritual director. A true spiritual director won't tell you what to do or how to do it, but they will turn you towards the Lord and remind you we are created in His image and likeness. That fact is comforting, but certainly leaves us with many questions as we live our day to day lives. Simply put, that is the point. If we had all the answers, we wouldn't turn towards the Lord to ask Him where to go, what to do, or how to do it. That is why when we are lost, spiritual direction is the best place to start.

Thank you, Fr. Tom Heron, for leading my soul back to Jesus and teaching me to continue to live in wonder and in awe of the divine mystery.

Angelina Heyse
1/7/24

A grateful testimony to the gift of spiritual direction, pointing hearts toward wonder, not perfection.

"Spiritual Direction," she says, "is not meant for learning how to perfectly pursue the Catholic faith or find the exact path to Heaven. My best answer to what Spiritual Direction is to those who ask is it is a journey and a space to learn and ask questions."

Therefore, I challenge you to reflect internally and to discern. Examine how God calls you to share these gifts with others.

The act of writing is but one powerful way to illuminate and preserve what matters most. Writing allows us to reflect on the experiences that define us, to articulate the truths we hold dear, and to share them with those we love. It is a means of connection across generations, across time, and across the heart's deepest divides.

These gifts, nurtured in the sacred space of our relationships with fellow Christ followers, find unique expression when shared with family. In writing to those closest to us, we not only preserve memories but also build bridges of faith and understanding that can deepen our bonds and anchor us in God's enduring love even when we may not agree 100 percent of the time.

CHAPTER 8

Family Ties

THE HEARTFELT ART OF WRITING TO YOUR LOVED ONES

Family relationships are a tapestry of shared experiences, both joyful and sorrowful, woven together by the bonds of that very truth we explored in the previous chapter: faith, memory, and love. These bonds shape us, define us, and remind us of the sacred gift of belonging. Reflecting on my journey as a spiritual mentor, I see that much of the wisdom I have been blessed to share with others was first nurtured within the context of my family. It is within the family —the first school of love—that we learn how to communicate, how to forgive, how to celebrate, and how to carry one another's burdens.

In quiet solitude, I reflect upon how the smallest gestures and simplest words have left indelible marks on my soul. One of the most significant moments of my early life came when I was just four and a half years old, standing beside my father in the front seat of his 1955 Mercury. He had taken me along to pick up supplies for his corner delicatessen, and as we stopped at a red light, he turned to me and said, "Tom, I want you to be my business partner." In that brief exchange, I felt something erupt within me. It was a sense of love and purpose that I couldn't articulate then, but has stayed with me for a lifetime.

What a powerful gift it is to know you are loved and that your life matters! Through his actions—holding my wrist as he taught me how to stamp cans, showing me how to turn them to face outward—I learned that the smallest gestures can carry sacramental significance. His words and actions became vessels of grace, forming my mind, heart, and soul in ways that continue to shape how I live and minister today.

The bonds we share with our families often hold a unique power to form and reform us. My mother, for instance, had a quiet but enduring way of nurturing our family through her written words. Each year on our birthdays, she would pen a simple note in a card for each of her children. They were never long or elaborate, but they carried a depth of love that words often fail to capture. She also corresponded regularly with her sisters, particularly her youngest, Marie and Joan. Though she spoke to her older sister, Ceil, on the phone almost daily, it was her letters to Marie and Joan that seemed to have a lasting impact. Perhaps it was because all four—Dot, Ceil, Marie, and Joan—were widows, bound by shared experiences of loss, that their written words became a lifeline for one another.

Dear Tom,

Happy 21st
I thank God for
blessing me with a
son who is a good
and holy priest
Thank you for
all your spiritual
& and financial
help I love you
very much.
Prayers and peace
Mom

*Hope you see something wonderful
everywhere you look,
hope you find something happy
every day of your lives.*

Dear Tom, Happy 21st. I thank God for blessing me with a son who is a good and holy priest. Thank you for all your spiritual & financial help. I love you very much. Prayers and peace, Mom

Unlike a phone call, which passes like a fleeting moment, a letter has a permanence that allows it to be read and re-read, its meaning deepening over time. My mother's letters reminded me that the act of writing is not just a means of communication; it is a way of affirming the worth of the recipient, of saying, "You are worth my time, my thought, and my effort."

This idea echoes throughout the Gospels, though strikingly, Jesus is recorded writing only once, in the sand, when the scribes and Pharisees brought before Him a woman caught in adultery. In that moment of tension and condemnation, He did not join the crowd's hostility. Instead, He knelt and wrote in the dust. We don't know what He wrote, but His action calmed the mob and turned their hearts away from judgment. Then He spoke words of enduring love and mercy to the woman: “Has no one condemned you? ... Neither do I.” (John 8:10-11).

What Jesus teaches us here is that words, whether spoken or written, can be transformative when they come from a place of love. They can diffuse anger, heal wounds, and open the door to new life. I often think of this when I consider the letters I’ve received from loved ones over the years. At age eleven, my grandfather wrote me a poem for my birthday—“Tommy Boy,” he called it—which I still treasure today. The following year, he gave me a green money bag with a note: “Tommy Lad, put all your money in this bag, but don’t let it get filled up. If someone’s around who needs it, you give them from your savings.” These simple words became touchstones for how I understood generosity and stewardship. By the way, I’m still in possession of that precious gift!

Family is the foundation upon which these values are built. My mother’s side of the family held annual reunions, gatherings filled with uproarious laughter that still echo in my soul. While the cousins played sports, the adults sat together, their laughter ringing out in joyful bursts. That laughter planted seeds of hope and joy within me, a reminder that even in the midst of life’s struggles, love has the power to uplift and sustain.

The relationships we have with our parents, siblings, and extended family members each carry their own unique dynamics, shaped by the roles we play in one another’s lives. As children, we look to our parents for guidance, protection, and affirmation. As siblings, we learn the give-and-take of shared life, its conflicts and reconciliations, its joys and sacrifices. As we grow older, these roles often shift, and we find ourselves becoming mentors to those who once guided us or seeking wisdom from those we once thought we knew completely.

These shifting dynamics remind us that family is not static; it is a living, breathing organism, constantly evolving yet rooted in love. Writing, whether in the form of letters, notes, or even shared stories, becomes a way of preserving these connections. It allows us to articulate what we might struggle to say aloud, to reflect on the experiences that shape us, and to leave a lasting legacy for those who come after us.

The act of writing is also an act of surrender; a recognition that our words, once shared, take on a life of their own. In the same way that my father's simple words at that red light have echoed through my life, so too can our words carry meaning far beyond what we intend.

Our relationships with our families take on an added layer of intimacy and complexity. Every family, in its imperfections and grace, is a reflection of the divine family—Father, Son, and Holy Spirit—and that in our love for one another, we mirror the love of the Blessed Trinity Itself.

WE ARE BOUND BY GRATITUDE, FAITH, AND CONNECTION

My mother had a gift for expressing gratitude, not only in her actions but also in her words. She understood the power of taking time to acknowledge the blessings in her life. She encouraged this in all of us, particularly through her tradition of marking special occasions with a personal touch. Birthdays in our household were not just about cake and candles; they were moments punctuated by handwritten notes, filled with warmth and love, reminding us of our worth.

Her encouragement extended far beyond celebrations. She had an uncanny ability to offer guidance with both tenderness and practicality. I recall an instance after I delivered the homily at a funeral for a young woman in her twenties who had tragically taken her own life. My mother, sitting in the pew, made a cutting motion across her throat, which was her signal for me to wrap things up. Afterward, she gently told me, "Be brief, and people will love you. And if you can't be brief, at least don't be boring." It was advice that carried her signature combination of wit and wisdom, reminding me to respect the time and emotions of others.

Dear Tom,
Happy Father's Day
You've been an inspiration
to so many people.
as a priest Father.
I pray God will
always bless you
as he has with your
beautiful homilies
and compassionate
ways. I love you
very much. Love
Mom

Dear Tom, Happy Father's Day. You've been an inspiration to so many people as a priest Father. I pray God will always bless you as He has with your beautiful homilies and compassionate ways. I love you very much. Love, Mom

Even in moments of correction, her encouragement shone through. She knew the value of relationships and often went to great lengths to keep memories alive. My older sister Sue recently told me that during her eighth-grade graduation, my mother had her write the names of all 60 of her classmates on the back of their class photo. "You'll forget some of these names if you don't write them down," she had said. It was a small act, but one that reflected her appreciation for the relationships that shape our lives.

Sue shares my mother's love of writing, though her letters often reflect her own spiritual journey. Her path, like many of ours, has not been without its challenges. In particular, she had called off a wedding just eight weeks before the date. It was a decision that, while necessary, left her reeling. It was during this vulnerable period that she found solace in an evangelical prayer group, a community that rekindled her faith in a new and profound way.

Her newfound spirituality became central to her identity, and it poured out in her writing. Every letter, every conversation, seemed to circle back to scripture. She would quote Jeremiah, Psalm 8, or John 4, encouraging others to engage with God's Word for themselves. I admired her zeal, though I sometimes felt the sibling rivalry creep in. As a priest, I was aware of how our Catholic faith places equal emphasis on Word and Sacrament, whereas Sue's perspective, shaped by her evangelical community, focused solely on scripture. Still, her passion for encouraging others to read the Bible was undeniable, and I respected her commitment to sharing her faith.

Wednesday
July 31, 2002

Dear Tom,

Thought I would write to you because it will get there as fast as a call.

I would be glad to stay with Mom. I am available most of the week, except if Jack has surgery on his shoulder, which we should know something tomorrow evening, I hope.

I appreciate your writing to me. I agree that when we have our quiet time there is that time of quiet communion with our Lord. I think our senses are heightened most in the quiet. Jeremiah 33:3 says "Call to me, and I will answer you, and tell you great and unsearchable things you do not know." This is the almighty God desiring communion with us. Psalm 8:4 "What is man that you are mindful of him, the son of man that you should care for him"? Oh! how He loves you and me. →

Dear Tom, Thought I would write to you because it will get there as fast as a call. I would be glad to stay with Mom. I am available most of the week, except if Jack has surgery on his shoulder, which we should know something tomorrow evening, I hope. I appreciate your writing to me. I agree that when we have our quiet time there is that time of quiet communion with our Lord. I think our senses are heightened most in the quiet. Jeremiah 33:3 says "Call to me, and I will answer you and tell you great and unsearchable things you do not know." This is the Almighty God desiring communion with us. Psalm 8:4 "What is man that you are mindful of him, the son of man that you should care for him"? Oh, how He loves you and me.

What I cherish most about Sue's letters is not their theological content but the way they reflect her heart—a heart shaped by our mother's example. My mother encouraged us to write not just out of duty but as a way to truly connect. Sue embraced that lesson fully, infusing her letters with a depth of thought and care that is uniquely hers.

Cousins hold a special place in our family dynamic, offering a blend of familiarity and uniqueness. My cousin Roni is a shining example of how thoughtfulness can strengthen family ties. She has impressively devoted herself to maintaining connections with her extended family and friends. Her letters are a testament to her remarkable sense of gratitude and her desire to enrich the relationships she holds dear.

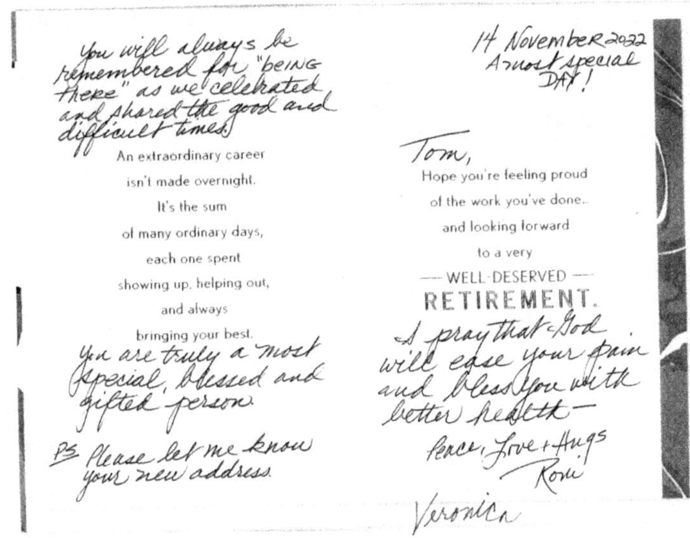

You will always be remembered for "being there" as we celebrated and shared the good and difficult times.

An extraordinary career
isn't made overnight.
It's the sum
of many ordinary days,
each one spent
showing up, helping out,
and always
bringing your best.

You are truly a most special, blessed and gifted person.

P.S. Please let me know your new address.

14 November 2022
A most special DAY!

Tom,

Hope you're feeling proud
of the work you've done...
and looking forward
to a very
— WELL-DESERVED —
RETIREMENT.

I pray that God will ease your pain and bless you with better health—

Peace, Love + Hugs
Roni

Veronica

You will always be remembered for "being there" as we celebrated and shared the good and difficult times. You are truly a most special, blessed and gifted person. P.S. Please let me know your new address. Tom, I pray that God will ease your pain and bless you with better health—Peace, love & hugs, Roni

Roni's letters go beyond the perfunctory "Happy Birthday" or "Thinking of You" sentiments. She takes the time to fill the space inside a card with personal reflections and heartfelt words. It's the difference between an obligatory gesture and a genuine attempt to deepen a connection. Her letters remind me of the joy that comes from truly being seen and appreciated.

Roni serves as a reminder that writing is a gift not only to the recipient but also to the writer. Roni's practice feels almost countercultural. Yet it is precisely this intentionality that makes her letters so impactful.

In a family, where dynamics are shaped by shared history and individual personalities, the written word becomes a bridge. It allows us to express what we might struggle to say aloud, to preserve memories that might otherwise fade, and to offer encouragement that lasts beyond the moment. My mother's bedtime tradition of saying, "Good night, God bless you, love you very much," encapsulates this spirit of intentionality. It is a small act, repeated daily, but it holds the power to uplift, to comfort, and to connect.

These lessons in love, gratitude, and thoughtfulness are not confined to family alone. They ripple outward, influencing how we engage with the world and with God. For if we can be intentional in our relationships with one another, how much more can we grow in our relationship with the One who created us?

BROTHERLY LOVE: A STUDY IN CONTRASTS

The bond between brothers is often layered with complexities that defy easy explanations. For my brother and me, those complexities were magnified by the shared absence of our father, a wound that left its unique imprint on each of us. While my memories of my father have been a source of strength and inspiration, my brother, who was only two when our father died, grew up with a deep and abiding void. This absence, which I have come to understand as a "felt absence," influenced so much of his life, including his struggles, his choices, and even the ferocity of his faith.

His journey through life has been anything but linear. From his battles with addiction to his relentless search for spiritual truth, his path has been marked by extremes. He has often embodied the principle that if you're going to do something, you should do it full tilt. When he turned to drugs and alcohol, he dove headfirst. When he left the Catholic Church and joined the Seventh-Day Adventists, his commitment was equally consuming. His hunger for meaning, for certainty, has always been both his greatest strength and his greatest inner turmoil.

Growing up, there was a fierce competitiveness between us, particularly in sports. He was a standout athlete, known for his strength and timing. Yet, beneath his physical strength and athletic prowess, there was a vulnerability, a longing for something he couldn't quite articulate, and a longing, I believe, that was rooted in the loss of our father.

One of the most vivid stories from his early years illustrates this deeply embedded sense of loss. Shortly after our father died, my brother, then just four or five years old, spotted a light blue '55 Mercury parked outside our home, the very same color, make, and model our father drove. He ran into the house, shouting with excitement, "Mommy, Mommy! Daddy's home!" My mother, trying to navigate her own grief while raising four children, had to sit him down and explain that it wasn't our father's car. The joy on his face transformed into a sadness that, in many ways, never fully left him. That moment, though perhaps buried in his memory, seemed to shape so much of his life; a longing for something lost and an anger at the God who allowed it to be taken.

January 29, 2002

Greetings in the Lord! As a follow-up to out telephone conversation today, I believe you said that you would be able to be with mom on Thursday evening and then return Friday afternoon at 4:00 p.m., leave on Saturday morning by 9:00 a.m. and return again at 6:30 p.m. I am most grateful to you for making this time available.

As you mentioned in our conversation, I was emotionally excited for the opportunity to speak with you even though we do not share the same Biblical, ecclesial or theological horizon. I would prefer an animated exchange to no exchange at all. I love you dearly and deeply miss regular contact with you.

Reflecting on our telephone conversation I have a question for you. If the flesh is totally corrupt, foul and putrid, as you claim the Bible teaches, why do you or anyone who holds this position eat? I pray in the future that you will reference our Lord and Savior Jesus Christ much more frequently than you reference Adam and Martin Luther. I also pray that we can continue our exchange and have more regular contact in the days ahead.

I have enclosed an article from the *Inquirer* that might be of interest to you.

"Doing nothing for others is the undoing of one's self" (Horace Mann). We must be purposely kind and generous or we miss the best part of life. The heart that goes out of itself gets large and full of joy. This is the great secret of the spiritual life. We do ourselves the most good doing something for others.

Dedicate yourselves to thankfulness. Let the word of Christ, rich as it is, dwell in you. In wisdom made perfect, instruct and admonish one another. Sing gratefully to God from your hearts in psalms, hymns, and inspired songs. Whatever you do, whether in speech or in action, do it in the name of the Lord Jesus. Give thanks to God the Father through Him.

Col 3: 14-17

With my brother, even small talk turns into Bible study.

That fury led to his rejection of the Catholic faith. He had a restless spirit, a need to push against boundaries. When he left the Catholic Church in 1989 to join the Seventh-Day Adventists was a declaration. He took down my mother's cherished religious artworks, including a painting of the Sacred Heart, a wedding gift, calling them idols. It broke her heart and left me outraged. My mother, who had dedicated herself to instilling the importance of faith in all of us, was devastated. She confided in me that she couldn't stay in my brother's home any longer; it had become oppressive. I helped her move into an apartment, a decision born of both sadness and necessity.

5 February, 2002

Dear Tom,

Greetings and Peace to you in our dear Saviour, Jesus Christ. Thank you for inviting me to serve Mom, it was very nice spending some time with Mom at the Lafferty home. Truly, there is an incomparable joy in serving others, and I pray for a fitness to serve others more readily.

As far as your question about sinful flesh, the key to this mystery is making the distinction between the body temple and the occupant. When Jesus casts out demons ,He does not leave the body temple empty but fills it with the Holy Spirit. Matt. 12:28,29. Christ bids all His newly created children to Watch and Pray less the evil spirits return and repossess the temple. Matt.12:43-45. The unspeakable gift of Christ in you the hope of glory must be maintained. Col.1:27.The flesh and blood body of man is mortal and subject to death regardless of who the occupant is; however only the body in which the Seed of Christ has been implanted can render a service to God, pass the judgement, and receive a sinless, immortal body.Ezekial 36:24-29 Romans 12:1,2 and 1Cor.15:42-58.

There is an excellent booklet on this subject entitled "The Three Temples" by F.T. Wright. If you would like a copy, let me know and I will gladly pass one to you.

And the verbal debate quickly makes its way to paper. We continue our banter while my brother hints at converting me!

His faith journey didn't stop with the Seventh-Day Adventists. Over the years, he moved from one denomination to another, each shift marked by the same intensity he brought to every aspect of his life. He ultimately became a Jehovah's Witness. His letters during this time of exploration were often relentless in their attempts to convert me. He believed that my role as a Catholic priest placed my soul in jeopardy, and he saw it as his mission to save me. His arguments were steeped in fundamentalist interpretations of Scripture, and he would marshal these arguments with the precision of someone trying to win a debate rather than foster a dialogue.

Sun. Oct 25, 2020.

Dear Tom,

Good Morning. It was enjoyable talking with you. You were in good spirits and lifted mine. As I Reflected on the memorys I asked God how I could help you. So here is God wants us to use our mental powers, to stretch them in the direction of future blessings.
Hope for the promised paradise earth
No one will get sick Isaiah 33:24
No one will die Revelation 21:3,4
No one will be hungry Psalm 72:16
Yes, everyone will have their own home
They will build it. Their own vineyards, orchards. They will plant it. Isaiah 65:21,22.
Faith and Hope are like twin sisters
By exercising faith in the Ransom sacrifice of Jesus Christ we are reconciled back to Jehovah and have His approval + blessing
The blessing is peace now in this wicked world and a bright hope for a clean, beautiful earth with perfect people worshipping God forever.

Agape

P.S. please take advantage of
jw.org a free online spiritual library

Dear Tom, Good Morning. It was enjoyable talking with you. You were in good spirits and lifted mine. As I reflected on the memory, I asked God how I could help you. So here is God wants us to use our mental powers, to stretch them in the direction of future blessings. Hope for the promised paradise on earth: No one will get sick – Isaiah 33:24. No one will die – Revelation 21:3,4. No one will be hungry – Psalm 72:16. Yes, everyone will have their own home. They will build it. Their own vineyards, orchards. They will plant it. – Isaiah 65:21,22. Faith and Hope are like twin sisters. By exercising faith in the Ransom sacrifice of Jesus Christ we are reconciled back to Jehovah and have His approval and blessing. The blessing is peace now in this wicked world and a bright hope for a clean, beautiful earth with perfect people worshipping God forever. Agape, [REDACTED]. P.S. Please take advantage of jw.org, a free online spiritual library.

At times, the letters were exhausting to read, filled with criticisms of Catholicism and impassioned pleas for me to abandon my vocation. I quickly realized that the source of the letter often mattered more to him than the content. Simply because it came from me, it was wrong. On more than one occasion, my brother told me he threw my letters in the trash without reading them. Whether or not that was true, it was clear that our correspondence was less about conversation and more about him asserting his position.

Despite the challenges, I continued to write to him. Writing was a way for me to extend grace, to meet him where he was, even if the gesture wasn't always reciprocated. His letters, while often abrasive, revealed a man grappling with deep wounds and searching for identity. His faith, though at times misguided in its rigidity, was a testament to his longing for something greater than himself.

There were moments when his struggles went beyond the theological. His addiction to drugs and alcohol led him to some of the darkest places imaginable. I will never forget the spring of 2009 when I found myself standing outside a drug house in Chester, praying for guidance. Inside, I found my brother, emaciated and curled up in the corner of a filthy room. It was a moment that felt like stepping into Dante's Inferno, a confrontation with raw evil that left me shaken. Yet, even in that darkness, there was a glimmer of hope. He walked out of that house with me, and while his road to recovery was far from straightforward, it was a step toward redemption.

My brother's life has been a study in contrasts: faith and doubt, love and resentment, strength and vulnerability. He is a reminder that family relationships are often fraught with complexities that defy easy resolution. Yet, he is also a prompting of the power of perseverance, of the grace that comes from continuing to show up, even when the path is difficult.

In recent years, his letters have taken on a different tone. While his desire to convert me remains, there is a sense of sobriety, both literal and figurative, in his writing. He continues to wrestle with his faith, his identity, and his place in the family. Our correspondence, though still challenging at times, has become a space where we can engage, however imperfectly, in the work of understanding one another.

October 18, 2012

Death and resurrection come as a package. When our attachment to our ego and its supports have been modified to such an extent that we sense a new freedom for action and new peacefulness with others, we can focus on others. However, our service to others is not subservient to "whatever you want." James and John might have got this impression from Jesus, and so they bluntly asked him to fulfill their fantasies. Jesus makes it clear that He is not available for that project and neither are we. Service means discerning the impulse of the Holy Spirit in the life of others and committing ourselves to their response. This commitment may bring us into conflict with people who are invested in maintaining oppressive, addictive structures. So in order to be faithful to service, we will have to "take up our cross." There is joy in being part of the Divine-human interchange that is fashioning a new humanity. It is the joy of the soul that soars when one cooperates with the invitation of the Holy Spirit.

Forgiveness is the key that unlocks the doors of resentment and the handcuffs of hostility. It is the virtue that breaks the chains of bitterness and the shackles of selfishness.

Your loving brother,

Even when we disagree, my compassion and love for my brother comes through my attempt at spiritual guidance.

I can see his journey mirroring the story of James and John, the sons of Zebedee. Despite their close relationship with Jesus, they struggled with their own unredeemed humanity, seeking prestige and recognition rather than humility and service.[26] Like them, my brother's path has been marked by a tension between pride and surrender, between seeking certainty and embracing the mystery of faith. And like them, he reminds me that the journey toward Christlike humanity is one of continual conversion, a process that requires us to die to ourselves in order to create space for the Holy Spirit to work within us.

Fri. July 17, 2020

Dear Tom,

Good Morning It's been some time since I heard from you. Are you still swimming? Great for the heart, easy on the joints As the human body floats in water. Me my exercise is Riding the bike and walking I truly pray to connect spiritually with you. The one way, a beginning would be to esteem the Word of God. Jesus is the Logos the spokesperson for Almighty God Jesus is God's only begotten Son the first born of all creation Rev 3:14 Get this piece of the puzzle and we'll have a meaningful connection. Thanks,

Dear Tom, Good Morning. It's been some time since I heard from you. Are you still swimming? Great for the heart, easy on the joints as the human body floats in water. Me, my exercise is riding the bike and walking. I truly pray to connect spiritually with you. The one way or beginning would be to esteem the Word of God. Jesus is the Logos, the spokesperson for Almighty God. Jesus is God's only begotten Son, the first born of all creation. – Rev 3:14 Get this piece of the puzzle and we'll have a meaningful connection.

My brother's story is far from over, and neither is our relationship. While the complexities of our family history and his choices will always shape our interactions, I remain committed to being a presence of grace in his life. It is a commitment born not of obligation but of love, the same love that binds us as brothers, despite everything that seeks to divide us.

BRIDGING DIFFERENCES AND AFFIRMING BONDS

Family is the place where love and values are learned and passed on, often without words but through the steady rhythm of daily life. My mother and father saw their role as parents as a vocation, one centered on handing on the faith that had been entrusted to them. My father, shaped by his Irish Catholic heritage, carried the traditions and beliefs of his family into our home in Darby, Pennsylvania. My mother, with her simple yet strongly rooted faith, nurtured in us a love for God and humanity that I have carried with me eternally. Their unity in faith was the cornerstone of their marriage, and nothing else came close to rivaling it in importance.

Within this foundation, my siblings and I grew up experiencing both the unity and the diversity that family relationships offer. Each of us carried the same faith, but expressed it in ways as varied as our personalities. Even when disagreements arose or relationships were strained, we remained connected by something deeper than ourselves.

My brother, for example, may have diverged from the faith of his upbringing, yet I often see glimmers of the same longing that animated my parents' lives, a yearning for meaning, purpose, and connection to the divine. His humor, which once brought a room of 500 to its feet at my ordination dinner, speaks to the joy and creativity that God places in all of us, even when it manifests itself differently. That humor, much like my parents' faith, reminds me that even amidst life's challenges, laughter has a unique way of disarming tension and revealing grace.

Reflect on the dynamics of your own family. What values, traditions, or stories shape your relationships today? How might you honor those gifts, even in the face of differences or challenges?

In writing to my family, I've found a way to bridge those differences, to affirm the bonds we share while celebrating the unique ways each of us carries forward the legacy of faith. Writing, whether serious or lighthearted, has the power to deepen connections, to heal, and to illuminate. It allows us to pause, to reflect, and to remind one another of what truly matters.

And sometimes, humor and lightheartedness can communicate truths in ways that solemn words cannot. Laughter, as I've witnessed in my family, has a grace all its own. Prayerfulness is but one part of the spiritual life. Playfulness is the other. Let's explore how we can harness that playfulness in our writing, as Jesus instructs us.

> AMEN, I SAY TO YOU, UNLESS YOU TURN AND BECOME LIKE CHILDREN, YOU WILL NOT ENTER THE KINGDOM OF HEAVEN. (MATTHEW 18:3)

CHAPTER 9

Through the Eyes of a Child

HUMOR AND LIGHTHEARTEDNESS IN WRITTEN COMMUNICATION

During my first Advent as a priest, I remember a conversation I had with a three-and-a-half-year-old in the back of the church. The little guy approached me and asked, "Are you God?" Perceptive little fellow, I thought.

"No," I responded. He snapped back, "Where is He?"

"Up in the Tabernacle," I explained. "How does He fit?" he inquired. "Can I see him?"

"No, he is locked up," I said. He burst out with a litany of questions. "Are you a cop? Why lock Him up? Did YOU lock him up?"

"I think I hear your mother calling you," I joked. He persisted. "Can you let Him out?"

"I don't have the key," I joked again. "You better let God out!"

We had better open not only the Tabernacle but also our hearts so that the Lord can not only come in but can also go out through us to love others.

--

From the intimate correspondence with family explored in the previous chapter, we move now to a different yet equally impressionable aspect of writing: letters shared with the youth of the Catholic faith. Writing to children invites us to embrace simplicity, joy, and a sense of wonder. It is not only an act of communication but also a way of fostering faith, nurturing relationships, and creating enduring memories. Jesus Himself reminded us, "Let the children come to me, and do not prevent them, for the kingdom of heaven belongs to such as these" (Matthew 19:14).

Children have a unique ability to view the world through eyes unclouded by cynicism or despair. They reflect what I often call great confidence, great simple faith, and wonder rather than worry. Writing to them allows us, as adults, to connect with that same openness and humility.

November 6, 2019

Dear Persephone,

Happy Birthday! Four years old! Wow! I pray that you will grow up and be as funny as your grandmother. She makes me laugh all the time.

Fr. Tom

To speak to a child is to step into their shoes and exhibit a familiar childlike wonder.

When I was first ordained, I made it a habit to write to children in my parish for their birthdays or other milestones rather than sending a card. I vividly remember Charlotte, a little girl who always wore a bow in her hair. Her mother once posed her on their front steps for a photo, acting as though she was reading one of my letters. I wrote to her and her younger brother, always ensuring that no child in a family was left out.

July 26, 2016

Dear Charlotte,

I am looking forward to cheering for you in the 2032 Summer Olympics in the swimming competition. I hope you continue to enjoy your swim lessons.

Your favorite best friend,

Fr. Tom

Fr. Tom

July 26, 2016

Dear J. T.,

I am very happy to hear you are feeling much better. Know that I am praying for you everyday so that you will be healthy and holy son and brother to your Mom and Dad and your big sister Charlotte.

Gratefully,

Fr. Tom

Fr. Tom

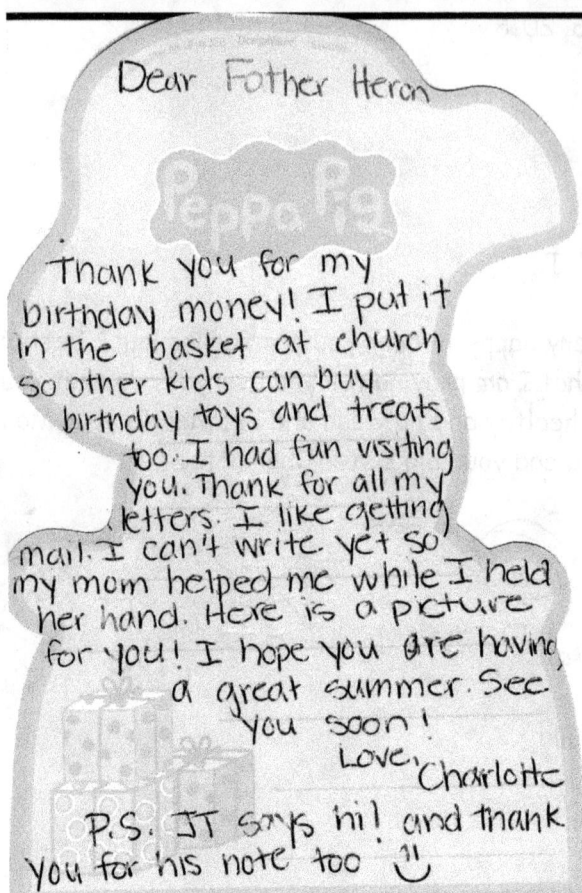

Dear Father Heron

Thank you for my birthday money! I put it in the basket at church so other kids can buy birthday toys and treats too. I had fun visiting you. Thank for all my letters. I like getting mail. I can't write yet so my mom helped me while I held her hand. Here is a picture for you! I hope you are having a great summer. See you soon!

Love, Charlotte

P.S. JT says hi! and thank you for his note too :)

This exchange was heartwarming, because not only are the children of the parish growing in faith, but their parents, too, are engaged.

Writing to children has its own rhythm and style. The letters need big print, bright colors, and something cartoonish to draw their attention. They also need a tone that balances encouragement and fun. For example, if a child learned how to swim, I might write, "Congratulations! Keep practicing, and maybe I'll see you at the Summer Olympics in 2032!" It's not just about acknowledging the achievement; it's about planting seeds of encouragement and joy.

Children are often more attuned to the present moment than adults, and celebrating their small victories reminds us to pause and find joy in everyday accomplishments. Their achievements, though small to us, are monumental to them. In responding to these milestones, I often found myself learning how to appreciate the simplicity of success. It's a reminder that even the smallest step forward in faith or life deserves acknowledgment.

Dear Nora,

Thank You for helping me proclaim the Gospel in Church and on the football field. I am grateful to you for your goodness and kindness.

You are a wonderful daughter, sister, and parishioner, and a beloved daughter of Father, Son, and Holy Spirit.

Gratefully,

Fr. Tom Heron

Encouragement is a key element when communicating with young parishioners.

These small gestures have a lasting impact. When I received letters or drawings from children, I made it a point to acknowledge them publicly in the parish. "Look what I got in the mail this week!" I'd say, holding up the artwork for everyone to see. Back at the rectory, I'd proudly display their creations on the refrigerator and invite their whole family back to come and see where their work was hung. These small acts told the children, "You matter. Your efforts matter. You bring joy to others."

Joy is not merely a fleeting emotion; it is a spiritual fruit, the result of living in harmony with God's will. Humor plays a role in this because it softens our hearts, clears our minds, and allows us to embrace life's imperfections. It helps us accept that we are all works in progress, growing into the fullness of God's love.

Children seem to understand this innately. They don't shy away from laughing at their mistakes, nor do they hesitate to celebrate the smallest victories. Their openness to joy teaches us that holiness is not about achieving a perfect life but about embracing the life we are given with gratitude and humility. We adults often forget that the ability to laugh at ourselves is a sign of spiritual maturity. It is a way of acknowledging our humanity while trusting in God's mercy.

Children often teach us as much as we teach them. One Sunday, during a dialogue homily, I asked a little girl named Nora if she had anything else to share. "Father," she said with a smile, "I love Jesus. And everyone should love Jesus." In that moment, Nora wasn't just speaking to me; she was preaching to the 200 parishioners sitting in the pews. Her simple faith and bold proclamation reminded all of us that the Gospel isn't meant to be complicated, it's meant to be lived with love and joy.

When preparing for a sabbatical during my time at St. Gabriel, I had a remarkable epiphany experience on a Saturday afternoon in a Genuardi's parking lot. I was waiting for a parking space to become available and a car parallel to me facing the other direction was waiting for one, too. As I glanced over to this car, a young girl with glasses, whose chin barely reached up to the bottom of the window looked at me and blew a kiss. I spontaneously reciprocated. Her face lit up in radiant splendor and joy and touched my soul in an unforgettable way. The little girl was mentally disabled. This experience convinces me that God asks us to be attentive to the simple and ordinary experiences of daily life and He will break in an extraordinary way.

Another time, while serving St. Gabriel, I was driving back from LA Fitness early in the morning. I stopped at a red light and glanced to my right, noticing a toddler with a mop of blond hair and a heavy jacket that covered his legs down to his ankles running down the street toward his father. The boy was full of delight and enthusiasm. As the boy approached, his dad bent down and they kissed. The boy, with great excitement, turned and started running back to his mother, who awaited his return. It was obvious to me that this was a family ritual. It re-emphasized the importance of ordinary rituals and how they enrich our lives. The Father, Son, and Holy Spirit desire to break into our routines countless times a day. That is why the Gospel imperative to be attentive, be away, be on guard, be vigilant is the first unskippable step in the spiritual life.

The sacraments offer moments to draw children into the mystery of faith. During baptisms, after lifting the child over the font, I'd often say, "You are a beloved child of the Blessed Trinity, and you will never be the same again." These words, spoken over an infant, echo the truth of our faith: that we are all children of God, lifted up by His grace. Family members would often comment afterward about how much this gesture meant to them. It's a reminder that humanizing a ritual opens the door for divine grace to transform hearts.

This gesture is inspired by the image of my father lifting me onto the refrigerator as a child. It is a visual reminder that we are all lifted by God's love. God continually lifts us, no matter our age or circumstance. These moments teach us that we are called not just to live but to live with a sense of awe and wonder.

Laughter is a gift that creates bonds and diffuses tension, making the sacred more accessible. In one story I cherish, a pre-K student, Amber, at St. Gabriel's told her mother, that her day was great after I celebrated mass with in her classroom. When her mother asked why, Amber responded, "Big Daddy came into the classroom today." Her mother asked what Big Daddy did, and she said, "Mommy, Big Daddy put Jesus in my heart!"

I could not wait to share this wonderful story with the principal. After telling her about Amber, she responded by saying, "Father, I don't want to burst your bubble, but we almost lost a child when you went into the classroom that day." She went on to explain that another child, Mary, went home and told her mother she's never going back again. "Why?" her mother asked. "He wet me and my Oreo cookie," referencing my ritual of sprinkling holy water on the children. Fortunately, Mary's mother was able to explain what it means to be blessed with holy water and Mary returned to pre-K the very next day. That taught me that no matter where you go, you'll always receive a mixed review!

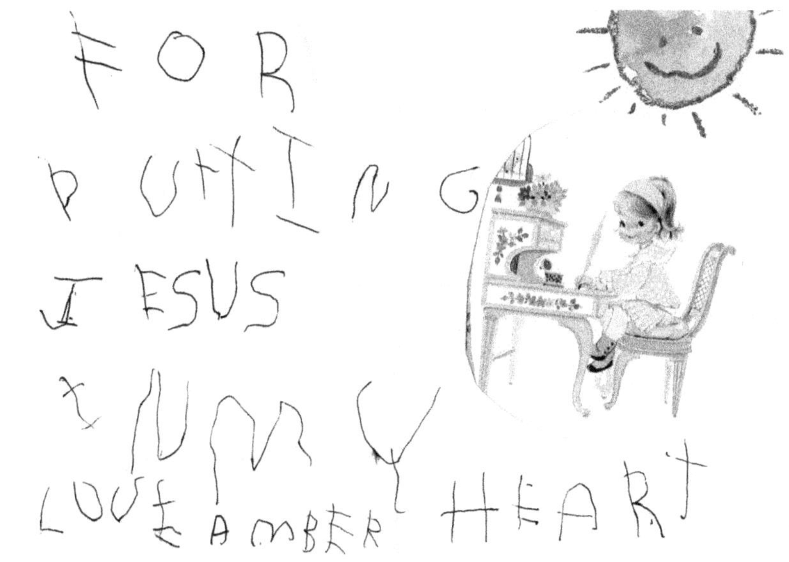
FOR
PUTTING
JESUS
IN MY
HEART
LOVE AMBER

For putting Jesus in my heart. Love, Amber

I've learned that laughter can humanize even the most formal occasions. At St. Michael's, I was struggling through a Mass with severe allergies. As I approached the final blessing, I sneezed … loudly. The congregation burst into laughter. I tried twice more to finish, only to sneeze again each time. Finally, I simply said, "Go in peace," and the church roared. In that moment, my humanness broke through the formality, creating a shared experience of joy.

The Four H Club—humility, hilarity, hospitality, and holiness—has guided my approach to ministry. I have always believed that laughter has an innate ability to humanize the sacred. A priest who can laugh at himself, or share a lighthearted moment, invites his parishioners into a more relatable faith experience.

Humor, when used in balance, helps break down the barriers of formality and creates a space for genuine connection.

Children, in their innocence, are natural comedians. Their letters to God, often filled with humorous questions and observations, are a treasure trove of wisdom and wit. Art Linkletter's famous show, *Kid's Say the Darndest Things*, where he asked children candid questions, captured this same spirit. Their answers, often hilariously unfiltered, reflected truths in their own way. Humor, I believe, is part of that Four H Club, after all: hilarity. It reminds us that while faith is serious, it's not somber.

Writing to children is about creating memories that shape their understanding of faith and community. Parents often sent me photos of baptisms, first Communions, and confirmations, accompanied by notes of gratitude. These gestures reveal enduring impact of the sacraments and the relationships they foster.

One mother shared that her child still kept a note I had sent years ago, tucked safely in a scrapbook. These stories underscore the power of written words to last beyond the moment. They become touchstones, connecting us to each other and to God.

Children have a way of bringing us back to the basics of life and faith. They remind us to find grace in the ordinary and to see the hand of God in small gestures and simple joys. Whether it's a baptismal blessing, a handwritten note, or a shared laugh, these moments reveal the sacredness of everyday life. They teach us that faith isn't just a set of beliefs; it's a way of seeing the world through the eyes of a child.

As we journey through life, let us remain attentive to the countless ways grace breaks into the ordinary. In laughter, in letters, and in the wide-eyed wonder of children, we find glimpses of the divine. As such, children, in their simplicity, teach us to trust, to hope, and to love without reservation.

The questions, observations, and humor children bring to the table pull us out of our routines and invite us to see life through new eyes. The exchanges I've shared have deepened my understanding of the Gospel. Through their innocence, children teach us that holiness is not about perfection but about openness.

How often do we pause to see the world through the eyes of a child? How often do we allow ourselves to laugh, to play, and to experience the joy that God desires for us? These are not trivial questions. They are invitations to rediscover the simplicity and wonder that are at the heart of our faith, which calls us not only to reverence but also to a joy that is contagious and transformative. By embracing humor and simplicity, we find a pathway to deeper connections with God and one another.

As we near this book's end, let us consider how we, as adults, can foster this joy within our parish communities. How might we engage our pastors and priests in conversations that uplift and inspire our faith communities? Writing is one way to create a dialogue that humanizes ministry, deepens faith, and builds relationships. May our words, like those of children, reflect a heart full of wonder and a spirit open to grace.

CHAPTER 10

Calling All Parishioners!

WRITING TO YOUR PASTOR/PRIEST

A priest I lived with on my first assignment lived his ministry in haste. He skipped many parts of the baptismal ritual. If there were more than five children to be baptized, he'd use a squirt gun to do the baptisms! He got reported.

The experience has to be a special one. It is the first sacrament into the Catholic Church, after all! I always call the name of the child several times in my baptismal ritual. The impression that is given that I have familiarity and so that it can be a memorable event for the parents, family, and friends. This offers connection with parishioners that inspire them to be more active in the church.

Moments of connection often open a window into deeper truths, allowing us to glimpse the beauty of our shared humanity. Parishioners, too, have the opportunity to extend an invitation to their spiritual shepherds to walk more closely with them on their journey of faith.

It's sometimes an untapped and forgotten mode of communication. It's one thing to chat with your priest in the rectory after mass. It's another to reflect upon how his homily relates to your own life and has touched you in ways you may not be able to express in a quick conversation.

Writing, after all, is a sacred act. Solitude and community are rooted in contrast, much like a longing heart and a listening ear. For me as a priest, these letters provide a window into the lives of the faithful and a space where they articulate their struggles, joys, and encounters with God. They also remind me of the privilege and responsibility of my vocation: to be a source of encouragement, a witness to hope, and a conduit for God's love.

One of the privileges of priesthood is that we meet people in their most grace-filled moments: baptisms, weddings, and even funerals. These sacramental encounters are not just isolated events but starting points for relationships. I've made it a habit to follow up these moments with a handwritten letter, an extension of the grace we've shared. In return, I've been blessed to receive letters that deepen my own understanding of the sacred.

March 16, 1998

Dear Fr. Herron,

Today you celebrated a Mass being said for my Mother, Mary Kane at St. Charles in Drexel Hill. The Homily you gave was such a comfort to me and I felt that God was speaking directly to me through you. You said my Mother's name with such reverence that I almost felt you must have known this wonderful woman but I know that you did not. She died last month at the age of 81 after a sudden heart attack and open heart surgery that she did not survive. I am the youngest of her fourteen children. We are all very grateful for God's goodness and for the gift of such a Mom, and yet the loss I feel is at times unbearable.

The ironic part is I do not live in St. Charles Parish and was very happy to be able to pray with some of my friends at the Mass for my Mom and when I saw you there I was very happy. See I met you once before and you touched my life in the same healing way that you did today. I was attending a Penance Service at my parish St. Laurence's in Highland Pk and I was standing in line for Fr. McLaughlin to hear my confession and this strong voice and feeling urged me into your line. I was thinking while I waited in line about the day my son was born and the words "Seek ye first the Kingdom of God" kept coming into my head no matter how much I tried to think of something else. When I knelt in front of you those are the words you said to me and I was so moved I could hardly speak to you but felt such healing and peace and that day you asked me to pray for your Mother, and now today you prayed for mine!

A few months later I was hoping you would return for my son's First Penance however I did not even know your name. Lo and behold you were there and you heard my son's first confession. This letter may seem like rambling to you but I wanted you to know that for the second time in my life you have been instrumental in healing me and I don't think it was a coincidence that you said that 6:30 Mass today. It was the hand of God and the words you spoke was the love of God and for you and my faith and God's goodness I am grateful and I just wanted you to know that .

God Bless YOU Father and Thank you,

Maureen

A priest never knows which homily, gesture, or moment of presence will become a lifeline of grace. Parishioners engage by showing up, listening, and allowing the Spirit to move between them.

This heartfelt letter was written while I was at Good Shepherd. The woman who wrote it had encountered me only in the confessional. She described how the way I spoke her mother's name during the liturgy left a lasting impression on her. She wrote, "You said my mother's name with such reverence that I knew, in that moment, God was present." Her words were a reminder of how a priest's demeanor—his tone, his attentiveness—can make real the divine love that people long to experience.

+
O

Thurs Aug 1

Dear Father Heron,

Just a note to tell you how beautiful the Mass, on Thursday for Mary [illegible] was. You did a great job, and homily, since you didn't know Mary or the family.

It was pleasure to read the first reading. I never did it before, I was honored, to read at Mary's funeral.

I never met Kathleen, til that day – but we talked on the phone for years. Since Mary didn't hear, for years, Kathleen spoke for her.

Good Shepherd has never left my heart, I had to leave 7 years ago. Sorry to say, my street got real bad. I lived at 6322 Allman St. My parents (Beers) lived 1740 S. 65th for about 50 years.

We just sold the house 3 years ago. She was in a nursing home for

2

4 years at St Frances. Luck to be 93.

I live in Our Lady of Fatima. It's a pretty church, but not like yours.

My children, as well as myself were baptized, went to school there, and were married from there. As I said in the 60's I worked at the rectory till I was married, and had my 1st children.

I know you heard of Father Donnell, I think those spirits is still in the walls.

Bless you Father, I wish I was in a position, to help you financially but I'm not. I live on my late husband Social Security.

Will always pray for you and all of your endevors. (Probably not spelled correct).

Say hello to Debbie, I know she is a wonderful help to you.

Sincerely,

Pat

Dear Father Heron, Just a note to tell you how beautiful the Mass on Thursday for Mary Heron was. You did a great job and homily, since you didn't know Mary or the family. It was a pleasure to read the first reading. I never did it before. I was honored to read at Mary's funeral. I never met Kathleen till that day – but we talked on the phone for years. Since Mary didn't hear for years, Kathleen spoke for her. Good Shepherd has never left my heart, I had to leave 7 years ago. Sorry to say, my street got real bad. I lived at 6322 Allman St. My parents (Beers) lived 1740 S. 60th for about 50 years. We just sold the house 3 years ago. She was in a nursing home for 4 years at St. Frances. Lucky to be 93. I live in Our Lady of Fatima. It's a pretty church, but not like yours. My children, as well as myself, were baptized, went to school there, and were married from there. As I said in the 60s I worked at the rectory till I was married and had my 1st children. I know your kind of Father Donnell, I think those spirits are still on the walls. Bless you Father, I wish I was in a position to help you financially but I'm not. I live on my late husband's Social Security. Will always pray for you and all of your endeavors (probably not spelled correct). Say hello to Debbie, I know she is a wonderful help to you. Sincerely, Pat [REDACTED]

Pat's letter is another that stands out in my mind. As a former parishioner of Good Shepherd in Southwest Philadelphia, she wrote to express her longing for the parish as it once was: a vibrant community of faith and fellowship. Her letter carried a sense of nostalgia, but also a desire to preserve the beauty of what she had experienced. She reminded me of a line from a song: "Let something remain."[27] It's a sentiment I often echo to parishioners, encouraging them to hold onto the memories that anchor them in faith, even as life changes around them.

Good Shepherd was indeed a parish of remarkable vitality, but it also bore witness to the challenges of shifting demographics and economic hardship, as we explored earlier. Pat's letter brought to mind the thousands of children who filled the halls of our schools and churches during my own youth. Those numbers have dwindled over the years, but the spirit of community and the legacy of faith endured. Her words were a testament to the power of memory to sustain us, even as we adapt to new realities.

January 8, 2014

Dear Father Heron,

Today I attended my Uncle Sal 's funeral at St. Cosmas & Damian church.

That was THE most amazing sermon in the catholic church I ever heard at a funeral, and possibly ever in the catholic church PERIOD!!! And personally, I needed that! Maybe that was a final gift from my uncle Sal, to orchestrate you being our priest today. I have been faithfully going to catholic church all my life, but lately have been wavering. I taught PREP for 10 years to third grade students & was instrumental in molding a lot of little lives. But lately I have been struggling with staying. About a half mile from my home a fantastic "new age, nondenominational church" has been built, and has been VERY successful in re-energizing the Christian faith around here....including my own children & husband. My husband was the last to buy in. He was raised catholic & went to 12 years of catholic school, but he too has been disenchanted with the Catholic Church. I have been disgusted with all that has been revealed in the Catholic Church over the last few years, and that has also really soured my taste. I even went so far as to call my pastor to discuss things with him, and after playing phone tag with him for a few days and him not having availability, I gave up.

So on Sundays my family goes to the "new church", and they sing & praise God, and hear these electrifying sermons and I have to be honest, it's pretty tough competition to the old ways of our long time catholic church. Simultaneously this "new church" was pumping them up & teaching them more than they ever knew about the bible; and the catholic church was boring them with their "unrelatable sermons" & their harsh unchristian rules. (I **did** notice that when you invited people to come up for communion today, **you DID NOT** specify "Catholics in good standing only" are welcome to come up). My husband and I have had countless conversations about this, and what would be a good solution to our "church problem". So on Sundays because I am just not ready to let go of the Catholic Church, I go to mass, and then drive over to the other "church" to join my family to hear the sermon from the reverend there. I love so many things about the catholic church. I am a HUGE Mary fan, and pray to her all day long, and this is one thing that I can't get there. So I did really appreciate you doing the Hail Mary at the cemetery.

When we say the "vocational prayer" in church on Sundays, I say my own version of it in my head. I pray for priest like you. Priests that are relevant, and caring, and know how to deal with real people. We shouldn't come out of mass feeling brow-beaten, and always falling short of what we should be. Your sermon was SO "spot on"....it was perfect in every way. At one point, my husband leaned over to me from down the pew & we both gave each other "thumbs up". My thirteen year old son, leaned into me and whispered, "Mom we need to drive 30 minutes away from home to come hear this priest on Sundays".

If I knew your sermon was going to be that good, I would've video taped it! If I didn't know better, I would've thought that you knew & cared for Uncle Sal for many years.....up to and including equating his name with the Savior. BEAUTIFULLY DONE!! I also appreciate you allowing my cousin and the grandchildren to eulogize Uncle Sal in the church.

Dear Father Heron, you may have single-handed kept me interested in staying with the Catholic church! I would very much like to come to some of your masses , and I will continue to pray for more priest like you!

Sincerely,

Kathleen

When homilies meet the heart, parishioners are moved to speak, and sometimes, to stay.

In 2014, I received a letter from a woman who had been deeply disillusioned by the scandals within the Church. She wrote to me because I presided over her uncle's funeral. Her uncle, too, had grown fed up with the Church.

Despite her anger and hurt, she found herself drawn back to the faith through small acts of kindness and connection. She wrote of attending Masses I celebrated and the gradual healing she experienced through the liturgy and community. Her letter was a poignant reminder that the Church, while flawed and human, remains a vessel of divine grace.

The courage it takes for someone to put pen to paper, especially in the wake of pain or doubt, is not lost on me. I always tell people that your presence in the pew enriches the faith community. Your absence diminishes the faith community. Everybody's unique and everybody's different. Don't think you have to become a cookie-cutter Catholic. No one person has the same type of relationship with God at a particular time in their life. Presence is essential.

3-1-2022

Dear Tom,

Thank you for coming to visit Dad today at Einstein. He has very strong and deep faith and your prayers today were meaningful and added a necessary support to his poor health. You are a blessing to our family.

In friendship and faith, Jean Kulp-Cucé

Dear Tom, Thank you for coming to visit Dad today at Einstein. He has very strong and deep faith and your prayers today were meaningful and added a necessary support to his poor health. You are a blessing to our family. In friendship and faith, Jean Kulp-Cuce'

In 2022, I received a call to visit the father of a woman whose family I had known for decades. I had celebrated her mother's funeral years earlier, and now her father was nearing the end of his life. When I arrived, I anointed him with the Sacrament of the Sick. The family's gratitude was palpable. Moments like these remind me of the sacred trust placed in priests to be present not only in times of celebration but also in times of sorrow and transition.

This visit, and the subsequent letters I received from the family, underscored the importance of being fully present in ministry. It is not enough to merely show up; we must bring with us the fullness of our attention, compassion, and faith. The letters I've received in return affirm that these efforts, however small they may seem, leave a lasting impact.

Dearest Father Heron ♥

Mike & I are eternally grateful for having met you. Today we were at church when you broke the news & we are truly heartbroken. It Brought tears to my eyes & when I relayed the message to my parents I could not stop crying! However in this letter I want to focus on all the positives you have brought into our Lives.

You have played a very VERY big role in us coming to church so consistently. We Love your messages & you are such a dynamic & Engaging Priest. You have played a very strong part in strengthening my faith in God! You have always been so happy & cheerful. Thank you for all your words of wisdom, your prayers & all your jokes. Thank you so much for marrying us. We could not have asked for anyone better to have married us. I Love how personable you are. 3:06 is when I walked up to Mike at the altar. I remember how big your smile was when I walked up. 3:46 is when you married us. I Remember the 4 types of Love you talked about. You have been an incredible Force in our Lives. My parents mentioned they wanted us to convey their regards to you & that you will be in their prayers. I Hope you know we are praying for you always. We pray for your Health. We will miss you terribly. Mike & I hope that we will still be able to see you on occasion. Please stay in touch. If we are Ever blessed with children I was hoping you would be the one to baptize them but I can take solace in the fact that our marriage was blessed by you. We truly do Love you & You mean so much to us. You will always be in our prayers. We hope to always stay in touch. Lots of Love, Roshin & Mike

* Please always know we are here for you in any way. Please don't hesitate to reach out!

Dearest Father Heron ♥ Mike & I are eternally grateful for having met you. Today we were at church when you broke the news & we are truly heartbroken. It brought tears to my eyes & when I relayed the message to my parents I could not stop crying! However in this letter I want to focus on all the positives you have brought into our lives. You have played a very VERY big role in us coming to church so consistently. We love your messages & you are such a dynamic & engaging priest. You have played a very strong part in strengthening my faith in God! You have always been so happy & cheerful. Thank you for all your words of wisdom, your prayers & all your jokes. Thank you so much for marrying us. We could not have asked for anyone better to have married us. I love how personable you are. 3:06 is when I walked up to Mike

> at the altar. I remember how big your smile was when I walked up. 3:46 is when you married us. I remember the 4 types of love you talked about. You have been an incredible force in our lives. My parents mentioned they wanted us to convey their regards to you & that you will be in their prayers! I hope you know we are praying for you always. We pray for your health. We will miss you terribly. Mike & I hope that we will still be able to see you on occasion. Please stay in touch. If we are ever blessed with children I was hoping you would be the one to baptize them but I can take solace in the fact that our marriage was blessed by you. We truly do love you & you mean so much to us. You will always be in our prayers. We hope to always stay in touch. Lots of love, Roshin & Mike. ➡️ Please always know we are here for you in any way. Please don't hesitate to reach out!

One of the joys of long-term ministry is walking with parishioners through different stages of their lives. When I announced my retirement as pastor of St. Matthew's in Conshohocken and eventual move to Holy Saviour in Norristown, I received a letter from a couple whose wedding I had officiated years earlier. They described how their faith had been nurtured during their time at St. Matthew's, where I served as pastor for nearly twelve years. From their first hesitant steps back into church to their joyous celebration of marriage, our journey together was marked by a shared commitment to growing in faith.

By that point in my vocational journey, I knew that I had given everything I could. My health was a major factor. I could no longer operate at my desired level of intensity, and I have no regrets about retiring. Dan Murray used to say, "Tom, let me use an image of a radio. You don't have to turn the volume up to ten in all the things you do. Sometimes, a five is appropriate." However, mediocrity was a major sin for me.

Today, I still say Mass; I still do weddings, but not with the volume. There were times at St. Matthew's when I conducted six funerals in eleven days. It's a tall task to do six funerals for six different groups of people, especially at my age. Plus, there were three men involved with the parish who, if a blade of grass was out of kilter in the cemetery, wanted to meet with me and speak their peace. You get tired of trying to thanklessly attend to those types of needs.

During my time at St. Matthew's, I merged four parishes into one. I also oversaw the remodeling of a whole school so that the building could be used for Catholic childcare. Not to mention weathering the storm of the global pandemic! It was one thing to another, and I was turning seventy years old. Every person I had grown up with had been retired for five, ten, or even fifteen years.

Roshin and Mike's letter reflected a theme that has recurred throughout my ministry: the transformative power of welcome. A simple greeting, a word of encouragement, or an invitation to engage more deeply with the parish community can spark a journey of renewal.

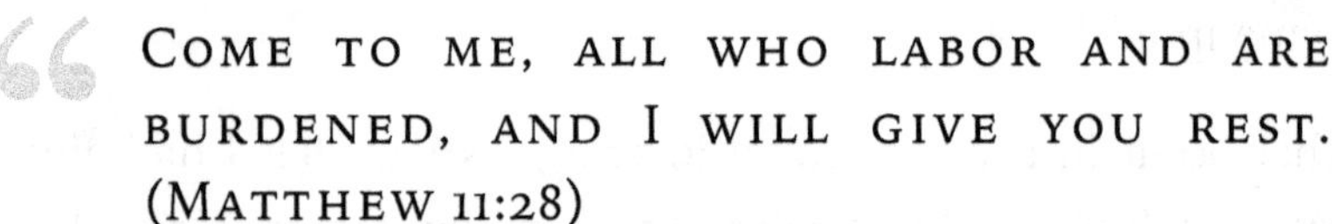

> COME TO ME, ALL WHO LABOR AND ARE BURDENED, AND I WILL GIVE YOU REST. (MATTHEW 11:28)

Our task as priests is to embody that invitation, creating spaces where people feel seen, known, and loved.

Rec'd 4/20/24

Hi Tom,

Thank you for the Article "Critical Grace Theory."

I had to read it about 3 times before I think I understood it, and even then, I don't know if I do. The Author certainly raises "critical Theory" to its broadest dimensions - as seen throughout history, including the Old Testament, and the christian process. He really emphasizes the Christian view of grace + forgiveness, and conversion of the heart, the concept of Love as well as justice. I agree with him that Christian critical theory is much more loving, personal, just, realistic and hopeful. But the author does say sin underlies unjust social systems. He does state that "critical Turn in modernity is incompatible with christianity because it takes a part of the truth and presents it as the whole truth." Which is true - but I do think modern critical theory does present some aspects of truth that need to be presented, thought about, prayed over and lead to some changes in our hearts, minds and state and church structures.

We believe God's TRUTH AND GRACE
is ABUNDANT, even Among so called
Non-Religious (secular) people, ideas, inventions,
Actions etc. – e.g. King Cyrus of Persia
sending the Israelites home from The Exile –
or Jesus – presenting the Good SAMARITAN – as
AN example of "grace" – so many examples back
Then + every day. – I hope This Author would
Accept. That There may be some Truth in
critical Theory (even if it's not perfect Truth)
And THAT if Justice is provided for God's
suffering people because of it – Then it can be
a presence of grace.

Well, Tom, I am heartbroken mostly The
past 2 years because of The Russia – Ukraine War +
the Israel - Hamas WAR + so much other violence + Hatred
in The world – BUT we pray + hope for God's
Kingdom + some human dignity + Love +
Mercy in our world.

Love you, my friend – Hope you are well.

Bill

Hi Tom, Thank you for the article *"Critical Grace Theory."* I had to read it about 3 times before I think I understood it – and even then I don't know if I do. The author certainly raises "critical theory" to its broadest dimension as seen throughout history – including the Old Testament and the Christian process. He really emphasizes the Christian view of grace + forgiveness, and conversion of the heart, the concept of love as well as justice. I agree with him that Christian critical theory is much more loving, personal, just, realistic and hopeful. But the author does cry sin w/ secular unjust social systems. He does state that "critical truth in modernity is incompatible w/ Christianity because it takes apart the truth and questions it as the whole truth." Which is true – but I do think modern critical theory does present some aspects of truth that need to be presented, thought about, prayed over and lead to some changes in our hearts, minds, and State and Church structures. We believe God's truth and grace is abundant, even among so-called non-religious (secular) people, ideas, inventions, actions, etc. – e.g. King Cyrus of Persia sending the Israelites home from the exile – or Jesus – praising the Good Samaritan as an example of "grace" – so many examples back then + even today. I hope this author would accept that there may be some truth in critical theory (even if it's not perfect truth) and that if justice is provided for God's suffering people because of it – then it can be a presence of grace. Well Tom, I am heartbroken mostly the past 2 years because of the Russia–Ukraine war + the Israel–Hamas war + so much other violence in the world – but we pray + hope for God's Kingdom + some human dignity + love + mercy in our world. Love you, my friend – Hope you are well. Bill

My correspondence with my longtime friend Bill Mattia spans decades. Bill and I first met in the seminary, and though our paths diverged, our connection remained. His letters often reflect the complexities of his journey, from the struggles that led him to leave the priesthood to the joys and challenges of his new vocation as a husband. In one particularly moving letter, he expressed gratitude for the support I had offered during his darkest moments.

Bill's story is a reminder that our lives are a blend of grace and sin, triumph and struggle. As St. Paul wrote, "For we are his handiwork, created in Christ Jesus for the good works that God has prepared in advance, that we should live in them" (Ephesians 2:10). Our task is to support one another in discerning and fulfilling the good works God has placed before us.

While Bill and I sometimes have conflicting worldviews, we admire one another's scholarly inquisitiveness. We often share articles with each other and discuss them after we've had a chance to quietly reflect upon them. This comes in the form of letter writing and it's a healthy exercise of the mind for us both.

Letter writing is an art that invites us into a deeper awareness of ourselves and others. Through the letters I've received, I have been humbled by the courage, vulnerability, and faith of those who have written to me. These letters are not merely exchanges of words; they are exchanges of grace, moments where the human and divine intersect.

I encourage you, dear reader, to consider the power of writing in your own life. How might a letter of encouragement, gratitude, or faith transform a relationship? What might you discover about yourself and others in the process? And if you feel so moved, I invite you to write to your pastor or priest. Share your joys and struggles, your questions and insights. You may find that in articulating your faith, you deepen it not just for yourself but for those who read your words.

Epilogue

THE LEGACY OF LETTERS IN OUR LIVES

"*Never underestimate the impact you can have on another person. Everyone should realize that they can be a source of grace in someone's life or a source of tragedy.*"

These words have lingered in my mind throughout the writing of this book, not as a warning but as a call to action and a reminder that each of us is called to be an instrument of God's grace in the lives of those we encounter.

Grace and sin are locked in a perpetual tug of war within the human heart, a struggle that begins early in life and persists until our last breath. At its core, this battle is a testament to our dignity as beloved children of God the Father, entrusted with the freedom to choose love over selfishness, humility over pride, and generosity over greed. But the reality of this struggle reminds us that we cannot succeed alone. We need one another. We need to be uplifted, encouraged, challenged, and reminded of the hope and joy that lie at the heart of our faith.

March 12,2023

To Whom It May Concern:

I don't really know how to start a letter like this. I'm not sure I'm quite from the generation of people that write letters anymore. But I feel, more than ever, compelled to publicly thank a man who, even though he didn't have to, filled in the blank spaces in my life both spiritually and physically.

I know my story isn't unique. My story is, unfortunately, one told too often by too many. Drugs, family torn apart, pain, anxiety, death. Whatever. Except, not for Father Tom Heron. See, I've learned in life that it only takes one person to show they are interested and care to change the life of a child for the better. Father Tom Heron was that one person to me. He nurtured my interests, challenged me to be better, and showed up to my performances. He was someone I could talk to, another male that could understand me growing up.

I am now 38 years old and I own my own contracting business because of the confidence he instilled in me. He was one of my very first clients when I went on my own. In his own way, being overly gracious and generous with whatever he has, this man has pretty much invested in me and my business. You can't stop him. Generosity is his love language. It just proves how much he believes in me... how much he believes in all of us really.

I'll end with this last thought. Father Tom Heron married me to my beautiful wife Lindsay, and he baptized both of my amazing daughters. I know he has affected the lives of many other kids just like me. Somehow, he has never lost interest and continues to be influential in my spiritual growth and now my daughters as well. The man leads with love. I'm pretty sure that's what we were initially taught to do.

Sincerely,

Pierce McKenna and Lindsay McKenna

Every soul lives in a daily tug of war between grace and sin. The junkyard dog pulls hard with noise and force, its rusty chain symbolic of the weight and wear of vice. The dove, ever gentle, lifts upward with hope, whispering of a higher way. We don't want to let go of either, but discipleship means letting grace lead, even while humbly acknowledging the weeds that remain alongside the wheat.

Letter writing offers a unique and powerful means of fulfilling that call. It is a simple yet deep way to build connections, share wisdom, and leave an enduring legacy. Every letter, whether written with a trembling hand or dashed off in a moment of spontaneity, carries within it the potential to become a vessel of grace to impact a life.

Jesus, in His boundless wisdom, often used stories to help us understand truths that might otherwise feel distant or abstract. He often challenged the status quo through stories that made His listeners question their assumptions about life, love, and holiness. The Good Samaritan, the Prodigal Son, the Woman at the Well—each story invites us to expand our understanding of what it means to love and be loved.

In the same way, the letters we write and the stories we share can serve as instruments of healing and inspiration. They invite others to see the world through a lens of faith, to recognize the presence of the Blessed Trinity in their lives, and to respond with courage and generosity.

I have learned this lesson time and again through my correspondence with parishioners. Whether responding to a grieving family, encouraging a young couple preparing for marriage, or simply offering a word of hope to someone in despair, each letter has been an opportunity to bear witness to the transformative power of divine love.

One of His most memorable parables, and one that is woven throughout the fibers of this book, is the story of the weeds and the wheat, where a farmer's field is sown with good seed but infiltrated by weeds. The servants, eager to protect the wheat, offer to pull up the weeds, but the farmer instructs them to wait until the harvest, lest they damage the wheat in their zeal. It is a story that resonates deeply with me, for it mirrors the complexity of our humanity.[28]

We are all a mixture of weeds and wheat, strengths and weaknesses, grace and sin. Like the farmer, we are called to approach our own hearts and the hearts of others with patience and humility. There are no shortcuts. Yet, it is precisely in our brokenness that we find opportunities to grow spiritually in the most powerful ways.

This book, born of decades of ministry and countless letters exchanged with parishioners, family, and friends, is a testament to the ways God works through our imperfections to sow seeds of grace. Each letter, each encounter, has reminded me of the great truth that God's love is always greater than our sin. It is a truth I have witnessed in the lives of those I have been privileged to serve and one that continues to inspire me as I strive to live as both a disciple and a shepherd.

December 28, 2024

Dear Father Heron,

A sincere THANK YOU for gifting me with your book "We Are Called". I was thrilled to receive it from my son, Sean. He said that you left the gym to get it for me from your car. It was a great Christmas gift, and one I will continue to enjoy reading for sure.

I am grateful that you wanted to tell and share the stories of the Lord's works in the lives of people you encountered during your 40 years as a devoted priest. I began reading your story of your remarkable childhood and your devotion to your Mom, your family and the store. Your Dad was a wise man to make you a business partner. You were an amazing child with gifts from the Holy Spirit evident in your actions. I learned your grandfather was a big influence and the storyteller of the family. So glad you inherited his ability to tell stories and share our Lord's stories in your homilies. We are grateful when you come to say Mass at IHM Church. You are very inspirational and a great teacher. We witness your love of God in your actions at Mass and your words that make for great conversations after Mass.... a true Disciple!

May God bless you always and grant you many more healthy years of serving him and touching the lives of those you meet. You are a wonderful writer so please keep up the storytelling. I look forward to continuing your book and learning more about your experiences. Thank you again. Happy 2025!

Sincerely,
Nancy Loughlin

Even a single story (let alone an entire book), prayerfully written and humbly shared, can travel farther than the author ever intended, sometimes finding its way into the heart of just one reader, and in doing so, fulfilling its sacred purpose.

. . .

One of the most humbling aspects of priestly ministry is the realization that God works through us, often in ways we cannot see. A simple gesture, a kind word, or a handwritten note can become the spark that ignites a transformation in someone's life. I think of the countless letters I have received over the years, some from strangers who were moved by a homily or a sacrament I celebrated, others from parishioners who felt seen and valued in a moment of vulnerability.

There was the woman who wrote to me after a funeral, deeply moved by the reverence with which I spoke her mother's name during the prayers of intercession. She admitted that she had been estranged from the Church for years but felt drawn back by that moment of grace. I could never have anticipated the impact those simple words would have, but they served as a reminder that God's grace is at work even in the smallest of actions.

Or consider the family who wrote to me years after a baptism to share how the ceremony had brought them closer to their faith. It was a day marked by laughter, tears, and a tangible sense of the Holy Spirit's presence. Those letters are not just memories for me; they are evidence of the profound ways God touches hearts through the sacraments and the community of faith.

As priests, we are called not only to spread The Good News but to live it authentically. Parishioners see us for who we are not only through the content of our homilies but on the credibility of our lives.

Do we practice what we preach? Do we speak with the authority that comes from a deep personal commitment to

Gospel Truth? These are questions that challenge me daily, and I suspect they challenge all of us who seek to live as disciples of Christ. Because authenticity is not limited to the priesthood. Each of us, in our own way, is called to be a bridge between Heaven and Earth, between the human and the divine. The letters we write, the relationships we nurture, the ways we serve one another ... all of these are opportunities to live out that call with integrity and love.

And I am grateful to have had the opportunity to perhaps impact just one life through writing this book. That's the whole purpose of doing this. If it impacts just one life, my cup will overflow with joy!

December 26, 2024

Dear Father Tom,

This is a note that has been waiting to be written since the third Sunday in Advent. but life had other plans. As I was sitting in Church I though back to a different Gaudete Sunday 39 years ago to early mass at St. James with Frank, Colleen and Megan Eileen which you celebrated. I so clearly remember words from your homily, "The world is pregnant with joyful anticipation for the birth of our Lord." They have never left me. I too was pregnant with joyful anticipation for the arrival of a new life. Little did I know at 8:30 AM that by early afternoon our Brendan would be born. While I miss your weekly reflections, this is an example that you are still preaching to me. Your words flood back to me often and images of baskets illustrating the miracle of the loaves and fishes as one example remain fresh for me.

I am sorry that your already fragile health has worsened and become more challenging. Know that I pray for you as you carry this cross when you would prefer to be in more active ministry. Every teacher knows that the seeds you plant will (hopefully in my case) reap great bounty in God's good time. You were the master sower of God's word.

In the Peace and Love of Christ,

Eileen Heron

To serve in Christ's name is to leave behind a legacy not measured in years, but in the souls stirred, the lives lifted, and the faith planted, often blooming long after the sowing is done.

In the grand relay of salvation history, we are the fourth leg of the race. The baton has been handed to us by our Creator (the Father), our Redeemer (the Son), and our Sanctifier (the Holy Spirit). Now, it is our turn to run the race with perseverance, carrying the light of faith to the finish line. It is a daunting task, but it is one we undertake not alone but in communion with the Body of Christ.

Are you willing to be that last leg of the race?

This is not the end of the story. It is an invitation to begin a new chapter, one in which we embrace the call to write, to connect, and to bear witness to the hope that sustains us. In the words of St. Paul, "Let us consider how we may spur one another on toward love and good deeds" (Hebrews 10:24).

To those who have shared this journey with me, thank you. Your letters, your stories, and your faith have been a source of immense joy and inspiration in my life. And to those who are just beginning to explore the power of the written word, I encourage you: Pick up the pen. Write the letter. Share your heart. You may never know the impact your words will have, but trust that God will use them in ways beyond your imagination.

Let us run the race together, hand in hand, letter by letter, word by word, until we meet in the eternal embrace of the Father, the Son, and the Holy Spirit.

Afterword

THE UNEXAMINED LIFE IS NOT WORTH LIVING

Unlike many of the great orators, such as Socrates and Jesus, who inspired their students and disciples with their eloquence but left no written record of their wisdom, St. Paul's words and thoughts have come down through history to us in large measure in his more than a dozen letters contained in the New Testament. In addition, his missionary labors and his teaching fill a significant amount of the book known as the Acts of the Apostles. These pages form nearly half of the New Testament, so much so, that St. Paul has been called the second founder of the Christian faith.

The character and personality of St. Paul have long been subjects of absorbing interest and endless research, while his life is one of the most colorful and dramatic of all the missionaries of Jesus. His message is of great interest today, two thousand years later.

Spoken words are fleeting, written words remain.

Many insights are discovered by an author's letter writing. Letters have the power to plumb the depths of our minds and hearts and expand our horizons. They reveal motivation and deepen understanding. What would the world be like without letters? We are at an inflection point of replacing letters with email, texts, and social media. The speed and convenience of technology in today's world seem a better alternative. In my judgment, something dehumanizing gets terribly lost with this option.

The letters John Adams and Abigail, his wife, sent to each other are priceless. There is a humaneness and integrity in letters that is lacking in other forms of written communication. One of the oldest surviving works of literature still read and studied, of course, is Homer's Iliad.

I write in order to listen more deeply to what is going on inside me and around me. Some days seem to be filled with pain and emptiness. No meaning. On other days, excitement and joy dominate. I see differently, hear differently. I taste, touch, and smell things differently, and that says a lot when battling celiac disease!

As I toiled over the work to be done in preparing for and writing this book, I wrestled with the question, "Am I writing this book for the glory of the Trinity and to help others along the way, or am I writing for my own glory?" We are all in search of home if only a home inside of us. Even in a resurrected order of living—especially in a resurrected order of living—dark times still show up to disrupt, distrub, and distract.

I am grateful for the days I can "taste and see the goodness of the Lord." When it is all said and done, all days—difficult and delightful—are graced moments because life itself is "full of grace." If only I can adjust the inner lens of my mind, heart, and soul. I now know, as I have just turned seventy-two, that it takes spiritual maturity to see, taste, and hear when I am in my down days.

Yet, writing continues to fuel me. I might be retired, but I'm always eager to pick up a pen and write. Letter writing will never leave me. No, not until my earthly duties are complete.

Therefore, I leave you with my latest Letter to the Editor because, in the chaotic political climate we live in today, it is easy for Christ's followers to forget His words. The bustle of our rapidly paced world and the noise of the twenty-four-hour news cycle and social media can certainly drown out the REAL (not fake) Good News. This letter urges you, a beloved friend of Christ, to recognize the Risen Lord in every person and live according to the Corporal and Spiritual Works of mercy. These same patterns that existed in Jesus's time are still in our time, and we are all called to respond as he instructed us to.

Letter to the Editor 11-20-2024

Jesus clearly instructs us to care, first and foremost, for the lost (religious and political leaders), the least (unborn babies in the womb), and the last (323,000 migrant children lost in our country) among you.

Jesus also informed his disciples to welcome the " poorest of the poor". When you show compassion, mercy, forgiveness, and generosity to the littlest (Zacchaeus LK19 :1-10), the least (unborn), the lost (Prodigal Son/ hurricane victims) and the last (323,000 migrant children in the U.S.) you extend the same compassion, mercy, forgiveness, and generosity to me.

Let us all pray that we can be united to living the truth of Jesus' teaching in St. Matthew's Gospel chapter 25: 31-45 today.

All disciples of the Risen Lord are called to order their lives according to the Corporal and Spiritual Works of Mercy.

Fr. Tom Heron

Acknowledgments

My third book, *Sacred Echoes of Faith,* has been a labor of love for me. I owe a great debt of gratitude to Kevin Haslam and Mary Kay McKenna for their support, goodwill, guidance, and patience in making this book possible. I am also thankful to my good friend, Bill Mattia, for reading the draft of the book and offering comments that helped improve the final copy. I bear any blame for faults or mistakes that persist in the book despite the best efforts of Kevin, Mary Kay, and Bill.

About the Author

Father Tom Heron is a Catholic priest serving the Archdiocese of Philadelphia, where he has served faithfully for more than four decades. Born in Darby, Pennsylvania, and raised in a close-knit Irish Catholic household in Collingdale, Pennsylvania, Father Tom's early life was shaped by the faith of his parents, who instilled in him a sense of devotion and community within the church. He was ordained in 1978 and has dedicated his ministry to parish work, teaching, spiritual direction, and the pastoral care of countless individuals and families.

A gifted communicator, Father Tom combines his deep theological understanding with a natural storytelling ability inherited from his Irish roots, namely, his grandfather. His homilies and writings are characterized by their accessibility, wisdom, and humor. Father Tom is the author of two previous books, *We Are All Called: Four Key Births We Are Invited to Experience as Disciples of the Lord* (2018) and *An Introductory Guide to Spiritual Maturity* (2021). Both works reflect his lifelong passion for helping others grow in their relationship with Father, Son, and Holy Spirit through personal reflection, prayer, and the sacraments.

Father Tom's priesthood has taken him to several parishes across the Archdiocese, where he has been praised for his approachability, his dedication to liturgical excellence, and his heartfelt engagement with parishioners of all ages. In addition to his parish duties, he spent time as a faculty member, inspiring young minds in Catholic education with his love of Scripture and his commitment to forming disciples.

In his downtime, Father Tom is an avid basketball enthusiast, gym-goer, and swimmer. He is a devout Philadelphia Eagles fan and often reflects on how teamwork, discipline, and perseverance are essential both on the field and in living a life of faith.

Now retired, Father Tom continues to serve the faith community at Holy Saviour Roman Catholic Church in Norristown, Pennsylvania, through Masses, weddings, and spiritual counsel, always bringing his characteristic warmth and sincerity to every encounter. Through his ministry and his writings, Father Tom Heron remains committed to his calling: helping others discover the joy and peace of living in God's grace.

Other Works by Father Tom

WE ARE ALL CALLED

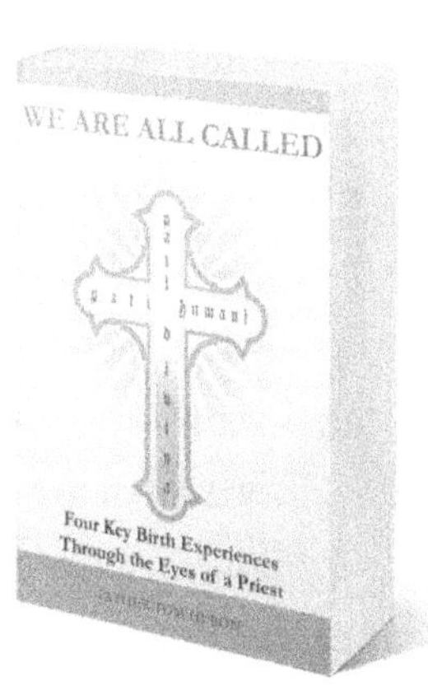

We Are All Called is the culmination of a series of life experiences for Father J. Thomas Heron, forty-plus years a priest. When Fr. Heron was just four years old, his dad died of heart failure. This significant life event forced Fr. Heron to mature at a young age, but also led him to ask many important questions. Had it not been for the vital spiritual and vocational mentors in his life, he may have never learned how to cope with tragedy and death—which he has now seen many times over—with grace and goodness. Fr. Heron believes in e.e. cummings' mantra, "we cannot be born enough"—that we all experience many births in life, and that we are all called by the Blessed Trinity to realize our places in salvation history, while carrying out our personal destinies. He is hopeful you will shed tears of joy and tears of empathy as you read his collection of stories, and ultimately realize many truths in your own life.

AN INTRODUCTORY GUIDE TO SPIRITUAL MATURITY

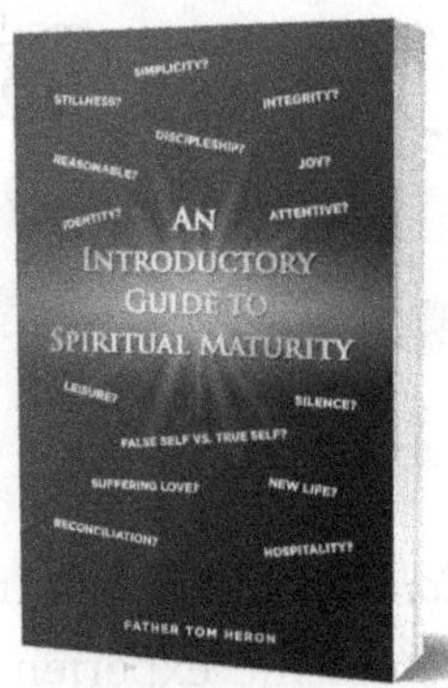

According to Father Tom Heron, the spiritual journey may be viewed through the prism of life experience and the meanings and virtues that involve many core elements, which are often difficult to see and discern in everyday life. Any mature spiritual adventure that tries to avoid these unavoidable challenges will be laden with trouble at some point or another. Change is challenging. Spiritual maturity takes a long time. There are no shortcuts. Today, everyone needs to find a spirituality that can live and grow in the midst of chaos and apparent absurdity. How well can you embrace uncertainty and live with risk? *An Introductory Guide to Spiritual Maturity* unmasks the concept of mature spirituality as the response of human freedom to the impulse of the Holy Spirit within us all and that which is all around us. For Christians, this encounter involves the person of Jesus, not as a historical figure of the past, but as the resurrected Lord in the present.

Appendix

EYES OF THE HEART

I hadn't yet been ordained. It was 1975, and I was a seminarian —green, restless, and hungry to serve. That year, I was assigned to St. Agatha–St. James, right at 38th and Chestnut in West Philadelphia. The assignment was simple enough: teach in the parish grade school, make a few visits to homebound parishioners. But the pastor in charge of the apostolate didn't think much of my presence. Every week at lunch, he'd tell Dan Dougherty and me to leave the seminary. Maybe it was a spiritual test. Maybe it was just old-school roughness. Either way, I found myself walking the streets, looking for where the Spirit might break in.

That's when I stumbled upon the Pennsylvania Women's Home for the Blind. I walked up, rang the bell, and asked the staff if there were anyone who might welcome a visitor. Without hesitation, they pointed me to the fourth floor.

Her name was Irma Rutherford.

Sept. 16, 1975,

Dear Wonderful Tom:

Thank you so much once again for a lovely day.' You know what it means to me to go to church; and especially with you. I enjoyed being in your parish. And then to go to your home and be with your dear family. How I loved sitting and chatting with Grnadma. Your mother worked much too hard getting dinner, but it was sure delicious. I enjoyed the pound cake since I'm home, but I still have the cup cakes to devour. Never mind, the time will come. It was so wonderful listening to the broadc st from Rome on the canoniz at on of Mother Seton to Sainthood. Eve ything was pervec t.

Please remember me to Bill and John; I hope I see them again sometime. Oh and dear Carmen; I don't want to forget him.

Hoping to see you soon, and best success with your studies. I am praying for you.

Expect to be up in the Poconos for the week- end. Isn't that fantastic, Florence just called me today and invited me for the week-end. Am really thriled about it.

My love to your family, and next time hope I see Suzanne.

My best love to you,

Your devoted friend,

Irma.

The moment I stepped into her room and heard her voice, I knew I had found someone special. Blind as she was, Irma radiated energy, wit, and delight. Her voice danced, bright and disarming. We hit it off instantly. I asked her if she had plans for Thanksgiving. She didn't. So I picked her up and brought her to Collingdale, where my mother lived. I wasn't even ordained, just a seminarian with a car and an instinct that people like Irma shouldn't be alone during holidays.

We kept visiting. Thursdays became our shared ministry, not just an assignment, but a rhythm of joy. Her blindness didn't limit her spirit. In fact, it sharpened her perception. Her joy had texture. Her words had warmth. And somewhere in all that, I learned to listen in a new way.

Oct. 9, 1981.

Dear FFathheTom:

Where do I begin, I reached home safely with sister Miriam fully in command. May be she doesn't know he way around. I didn't have to tell her anything; no Market St. for he; right out Race to some Street that took us ro the Art Museum, and then on to 34th St. to Powelton Ave. My but she knew shere she was going. We were here by eleven o(clock. She came up and saw my room and liked it. I surely do appreciate her bringing me home. We had a wonderful time gogethr.

Fathe Tom, thank you for everything. I had a marvdlelous time. Words fail me,--at leasr I can put that, you know better,--to tell you how much I appreciated everything. I loved reading for you at Mass, and the rest was super, too. I loved going through school at such a rapid pace, and I value my special certificate,--your approval. I just thought each group was finer th n the one before. Everyone paid so much attention and seemed to love my bwing there. Please thank all t e kind teafhers for their permitting me to speak in their classes, and I hope I may do it again sometime in the future. I was so glad to see so many of the girls in High School I knew in eighth grade long ago. I only wish it could ome soon again. That's being a piggy, isn't it,

The hospitality of the Sisters was beyong description. I really thought I was somebody special even to myself.

Don't worry about your letters, Fa her Tom. I h ve them safe. I would just love to thorw them away, but know you would be crors, so better not do that.

Give my love to eve y one, and thank you again for all your wonderful though tfulness of me. I hope I may do something ag in for you. Tell the other Father I will read at his Mass next time for sure; I was a real washout. Will try to do better.

Lots of love, and thanks again. Hope you keep well and go on doing your wonderful work. But give yourself some time to rest, please.

Your friend as ever,

Irma.

By 1981, I was serving in Levittown, and I brought her up for a visit just to give her a change of scenery, and to let the parish kids meet her. That visit turned out to be a gift to everyone involved. Irma was lifted into something like glory. She rode that high for three or four weeks. You could feel the jubilation radiating from her, even days after. And when she sent a note afterward—one of those simple handwritten things—you could hear her rejoice, still singing in her script.

I've always been a handwritten-letter kind of guy. Even as my handwriting worsened with age, I still kept a pen nearby. I never liked typing. I'd write things longhand and have someone help me type them later. There's something in the gesture of writing —holding the pen, forming each word—that holds a piece of your presence. Irma understood that. So did I.

Her voice stayed with me. Not because she was blind, but because she saw. She saw people. She saw joy. And she showed me that sometimes, all ministry takes is a quiet visit to the fourth floor and a willingness to stay long enough to listen.

THE CHRIST-LIKE LIFE THAT SPANNED A CENTURY

Dear Father:
I intend to call the
Johnstons to thank them for
the check. As you know, they
did the same thing last year.
I didn't know that
Kathleen and Jim have a
daughter living in
Conshohocken.
Thank you, Father, for
the beautiful St. Matthew
plaque 1851-2001. No,
I don't remember 1851!

(2)

Also, congratulations and
thank you, Father, for
the great job you are
doing with the new
St. Matthews.
Sincerely,
Bud Reilly
Sorry you couldn't
make the party.

Dear Father, I intend to call the Johnstons to thank them for the check. As you know, they did the same thing last year. I didn't know that Kathleen and Jim have a daughter living in Conshohocken. Thank you, Father, for the beautiful St. Matthew plaque 1851–2001. No, I don't remember 1851! Also, congratulations and thank you, Father, for the good job you are doing with the new St. Matthew's. Sincerely, Bud Reilly. Sorry you couldn't make the party.

Every once in a while, you meet someone whose presence feels like a bridge between centuries. Bud Reilly was that kind of soul. A parishioner of St. Matthew's who lived more than a hundred years, Bud carried within him a quiet, enduring joy. He was a gracious man through and through, someone who knew how to live fully without needing to be loud about it. He never married, but he wasn't alone. His life rippled out in the lives of relatives, friends, neighbors, and all of us who were blessed to know him.

He was born in 1919, the same year the current church building at St. Matthew's was constructed. We celebrated his 100th birthday in 2019, a century marked not only by longevity but by faith, humility, and generosity. He died in 2021, but he never seemed to grow old in spirit. Even in his late nineties, back around 2016, I remember thinking: "He's ninety-seven, but his gratitude could make a man half his age pause and pay attention."

Bud had a deep sense of legacy. His grandparents came to Conshohocken from Ireland in 1853, just two years after the town was founded. That family never left. They stayed rooted. Bud was baptized at St. Matthew's, went to school there, and gave his life to that community in quiet, steadfast ways. His niece still carries on that presence today. If the Lord allows, their family could soon mark 200 years of unbroken presence in the life of the parish, a remarkable echo of faithfulness stretching from famine-era Ireland to 21st-century Pennsylvania.

Bud once handed me a check—on behalf of relatives who no longer lived in the parish—but the gesture, like the man himself, wasn't about money. It was about connection.

We honored him with a plaque, but truthfully, his life was already a monument. He didn't need a stone to mark what he had done. The legacy was already in the walls, the stories, the pews he sat in, and the people he quietly supported. He lived the Gospel by living well. No fanfare, no spotlight. Just presence, fidelity, and joy.

There's something sacred about that kind of life. It's not showy. It's not headline-worthy. But it's deeply Christ-like. Bud Reilly didn't need to preach. He *was* a homily ... one that took more than a hundred years to write.

WHEN NICODEMUS MEETS CENTER COURT

Every once in a while, a student surprises you, not with grades or obedience, but with a kind of presence that stays. Joe Dempsey was one of those students. He recently sent me a thoughtful, generous note that reached me at just the right time. He mentioned I'd had some influence on him during his high school days at Archbishop Kennedy. That meant something. Not because it puffed me up, but because it reminded me that the seeds we plant in the classroom often bloom years later, unseen, until they surprise us in the form of a letter, a visit, a gentle word.

Joe was at Kennedy for four years, yet his name never strayed far from the Conshohocken community. People would bring him up, and he would show up, quietly slipping into Mass at St. Matthew's from time to time. I always made a point to ask about his teaching and his coaching. I was interested not just in what he did, but in how he did it. And with Joe, you could count on heart, humor, and a deep sense of responsibility.

Padre -

MK told me that you have been experiencing difficult health challenges. Given that you've spent your entire adult life, and ministry trying to inspire people - I thought I'd drop you a note to inspire you.

This situation is probably very similar to a recent memory that you can probably draw upon - the days when we would play one on one at AKHS. How were you going to stop me? How would you defend me? Where would you find the strength and the stamina? There seemed to be no answers.

You know, of course, being a life-long athlete and competitor, the solution lies in you! Your strength of character, your determination, your fight, your resolve, your work ethic, and of course, your strong faith! (I would have referenced your quickness, your ability to go by me, your excellent shooting, and your ability to dribble equally as well with both hands, but of course, none of those things existed!)

Back to your faith and resolve. You are one of the most determined men I have ever met. Unshakable, and unyielding. You are only in the 3rd quarter here. The opponent has punched, and perhaps you need a timeout. Finish this quarter strong - as the the 4th quarter and only the 4th quarter, will determine the outcome of the contest!

Stay well, and please know I've been thinking about you and praying for you.

Grateful to call you a friend!

Even as a student, he had the rare ability to hover between youth and maturity. He was playful, no doubt—quick-witted, clever, and often hilarious. It didn't take more than an eyebrow raise from me before he was off to the races, riffing on something that would leave the whole room laughing, or just at me at the very least. He didn't need a stage, just an audience of one. But beneath that charm was something more: a quiet dignity, a kind of inner clarity that could emerge without fanfare.

In that sense, I always thought of him as a kind of Nicodemus. He'd come to me—not literally in the dark of night, but with the same discreet reverence to talk about the deeper things. Family struggles. Personal crossroads. Questions about teaching. Life. Sometimes even halftime strategy. He didn't want others to see that side, perhaps out of humility, or a worry about being mistaken for a flatterer. I never saw it that way. What I saw was someone seeking wisdom and doing it with sincerity.

Over the years, our relationship naturally evolved. I followed him into college, attended a few of his basketball games, and stayed in touch. He would stop by Kennedy when I was still there, and later, he'd visit me at the seminary. We'd run into each other at the Palestra, the old sacred sports hall in Philadelphia, and pick up as if no time had passed. These weren't formal meetings. They were just moments of continuity and grace showing up in the ordinary.

One of the things I admire most about Joe is his ability to switch roles without losing respect. He could speak to me as a teacher one moment and as a friend the next. And when I hit a rough patch—yes, priests have those too—he had the freedom and the grace to offer encouragement. That's not something every former student can do. It takes humility, confidence, and trust.

Joe's a good man … a devoted husband, a committed father, a man of faith. Teaching and coaching matter to him, and he's poured himself into those vocations. But what defines him is what he's built at home. That foundation—of marriage and fatherhood—always superseded every other role. And yet, he brings the same depth and humor to a classroom or a basketball court that he brought into my class all those years ago.

It's one of the great privileges of priesthood: to see a student grow into his life. And sometimes, if you're lucky, he writes you a letter to remind you that none of it was wasted.

RESIST. PERSIST. NEVER GIVE UP.

In the fabric of Philadelphia's narrative, certain threads stand out: vivid, enduring, and intricately woven into the city's identity. Bill Lyon was one such fiber of the tapestry. For more than three decades, his words graced the pages of *The Philadelphia Inquirer*, capturing not just the events of the sporting world, but the very essence of human endeavor.

Bill's prose was a masterclass in storytelling. Each column flowed seamlessly from the first sentence to the last, a testament to his unparalleled gift. His writing was rich with allusions, drawing from poetry, the annals of Greek and Latin history, and the vast expanse of literature. He didn't just report on games; he illuminated the human spirit behind each play, each triumph, each defeat.

Letter to the Editor:

What do you do when blessings - an agile mind, efficient typing skills become burdensome? What happens when our bodies and our minds betray us?

The speed of hunt and peck is replaced by tremors that paralyze and handcuff Bill Lyon. Tremors also affect one's train of thought. Words that flow like a running stream, dry up and we can't seem to reach into our grey matter and pull out the one precise word we are looking for.

Again, the question remains, what do you do at this crucial crossroad in your life? Become depressed? Be passive? Give up? Throw in the towel? Or accept your limitations and come up with a new game plan.

Thanks, Bill for your courageous stance that inspires us to follow your example and lead.

"Resist. Persist. Never give up."

Fr. Tom Heron

As time marched on, Bill faced formidable adversaries with his health, primarily Alzheimer's and Parkinson's diseases. These relentless foes sought to dim his brilliance, making the act of writing—a task once as natural to him as breathing—a herculean effort. The man who once penned multiple columns a week found himself laboring to produce one per month. Yet, true to his indomitable spirit, he pressed on.

In his final articles, Bill adopted a mantra that encapsulated his life's philosophy: "Resist. Persist. Never Give Up."[29] These words weren't just a rallying cry against his personal battles; they were a beacon for all who faced their own trials. Even as his health declined, Bill's commitment to his craft remained unwavering. He may have deemed his later pieces subpar, but to those of us who read them, they were nothing short of inspiring. Even at diminished capacity, Bill Lyon's "subpar" outshone the best efforts of many.

Reflecting on Bill's journey, I am behooved to recognize the impact one individual can have on a community. His courage, resilience, and dedication serve as a testament to the power of the human spirit. Bill taught us that while our bodies and minds may falter, our determination can remain steadfast. He showed us that even in the face of insurmountable odds, one can choose to resist, to persist, and to never give up.

As we navigate our own challenges, may we carry forward Bill's legacy, embodying the perseverance and passion he so eloquently championed.

LOCKER ROOM LETTERS

Letters exchanged with sports figures (many with Phildelphia roots).

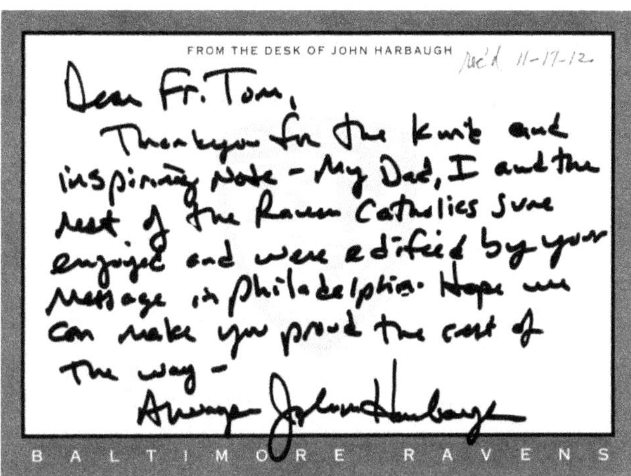

FROM THE DESK OF JOHN HARBAUGH

Rec'd 11-17-12

Dear Fr. Tom,

Thank you for the kind and inspiring note - My Dad, I and the rest of the Raven Catholics sure enjoyed and were edified by your message in Philadelphia. Hope we can make you proud the rest of the way -

Always John Harbaugh

BALTIMORE RAVENS

Dear Fr. Tom, Thank you fo rthe kind and inspiring note - My Dad, I and the rest of the Roman Catholics sure enjoyed and were edified by your message in Philadelphia. Hope we can make you proud the rest of the way - Always, John Harbaugh (former Philadelphia Eagles special teams coordinator and defensive backs coach)

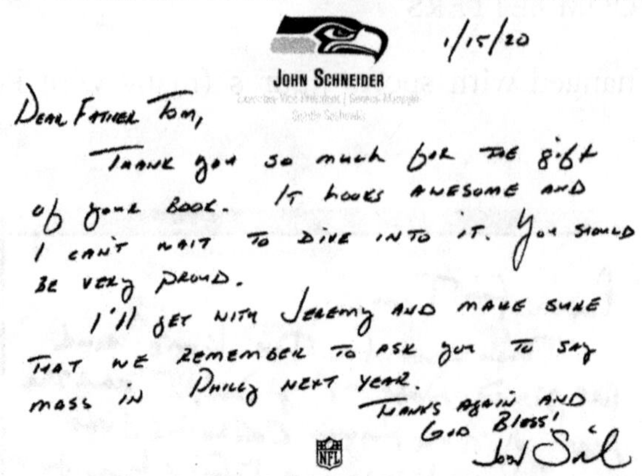

JOHN SCHNEIDER

1/15/20

Dear Father Tom,

Thank you so much for the gift of your Book. It looks awesome and I can't wait to dive into it. You should be very proud.

I'll get with Jeremy and make sure that we remember to ask you to say mass in Philly next year.

Thanks again and God Bless!

Dear Father Tom, Thank you so much for the gift of your Book. It looks awesome and I can't wait to dive into it. You should be very proud. I'll get with Jeremy and make sure that we remember to ask you to say Mass in Philly next year. Thanks again and God Bless! John Schneider (NFL executive)

11/18/19

Dear Fr. Heron,

Congratulations on your book. That's a wonderful achievement. You should be very proud. I see you are a Collingdale boy. We share Delco roots. I grew up a little farther down MacDade Blvd. in Folsom.

Thanks for thinking of me & thanks for the kind words. You might want to say a prayer for the Eagles receiver corp. They could use it.

Have a wonderful Thanksgiving. Best wishes with the book!

Sincerely,
Ray Didinger

Dear Fr. Heron, Congratulations on your book. That's a wonderful achievement. You should be very proud. I see you are a Collingdale boy. We share Delco roots. I grew up a little farther down MacDade Blvd. in Folsom. Thanks for thinking of me and thanks for the kind words. You might want to say a prayer for the Eagles receiver corp. They could use it. Have a wonderful Thanksgiving. Best wishes with the book! Sincerely, Ray Didinger (Philadelphia native and long-time Philaelphia sports journalist and media personality; Philadelphia Sports Hall of Famer and winner of multiple prestigious writing awards)

August 8, 2007

Mrs. Edward W. McCaskey

Dear Mrs. McCaskey,

Thank you for your recent letter of July 25, 2007. I certainly understand the changes that Coach Lovie Smith made regarding the travel schedule.

If the Vincentian priest is unable to travel with the team to Philadelphia, I would be available on Sunday morning, October 21 to celebrate Mass for you, the coaching staff, the players, and anyone else who wants to attend.

I wish you and the Chicago Bears the very best for the 2007 season.

"Many of you have already found out, and others will find out in the course of their lives, that truth eludes us if we do not concentrate with total attention on its pursuit." (Alexander Solzhenitsyn)

"It is a fascinating call to attend to and awaken that invisible dimension of life whence all things flow." (John O'Donohue)

Sincerely in Our Lord,

Reverend J. Thomas Heron
Pastor

A letter I wrote in 2007 to Virginia Halas McCaskey, former principal owner of the Chicago Bears and Drexel University alumna. She died in February 2025 at the age of 102

Reverend and dear Father,

Thank you for your celebra-
tion of a mass for my son,
Michal. Thank you for the
enclosures and your prayers.
I am also grateful for daily
mass on EWTN and for Releoan
Radio. Respectfully. Virginia
McC.

CHICAGO BEARS

Reverend and dear Father, Thank you for your celebration of a mass for my son, Michael. Thank you for the enclosures and your prayers. I am also grateful for daily mass on EWTN and for Relevant Radio. Respectfully, Virginia McC.

Works Cited

1. Pilkington, Ed. "Imagine: Lennon's piano on a peace tour." The Guardian. April 16, 2007. https://www.theguardian.com/world/2007/apr/16/usa.musicnews.
2. From the Headmaster. "The only real sadness, the only real failure, the only great tragedy in life, is not to become a saint." Chesterton Academy of the Holy Family. March 31, 2017. https://www.chestertonacademyoftheholyfamily.com/news/from-the-headmaster/the-only-real-sadness-the-only-real-failure-the-only-great-tragedy-in-life-is-not-to-become-a-saint.
3. 1 Tim. 1:3
4. Titus 1:5
5. Acts 15:36-40, 13:13
6. Mark 1:40-42
7. Mark 3:1-6
8. Mark 5:25-34
9. Col. 1:24
10. Noonan, Peggy. "The Wisdom of Oscar Hammerstein." The Wall Street Journal. March 29, 2018. https://peggynoonan.com/the-wisdom-of-oscar-hammerstein/.
11. Hemingway, Ernest. *A Farewell to Arms*. New York: Scribner, 1997.
12. Cleveland Clinic. "Fetabl Development." Accessed March 29, 2025. https://my.clevelandclinic.org/health/articles/7247-fetal-development-stages-of-growth.
13. Catholic Answers. "Ectopic Pregnancy and Double Effect." Accessed March 29, 2025. https://www.catholic.com/qa/ectopic-pregnancy-and-double-effect.
14. Jones, Rachel K., Friedrich-Karnik, Amy. "Medication Abortion Accounted for 63% of All US Abortions in 2023–An Increase from 53% in 2020." Guttmacher Institute. March 2024. https://www.guttmacher.org/2024/03/medication-abortion-accounted-63-all-us-abortions-2023-increase-53-2020.
15. John 10:10

16. Fraga, Brian. "DC's Cardinal Gregory criticizes Biden's 'cafeteria' Catholicism." National Catholic Reporter. April 1, 2024. https://www.ncronline.org/news/dcs-cardinal-gregory-criticizes-bidens-cafeteria-catholicism.
17. Britannica. "Horace." Last modified March 10, 2025. https://www.britannica.com/biography/Horace-Roman-poet.
18. African Studies Center - University of Pennsylvania. "Letter from a Birmingham Jail [King Jr.]." April 16, 1963. https://www.africa.upenn.edu/Articles_Gen/Letter_Birmingham.html.
19. Rom. 15:14
20. Kelly, Matthew. "The Secret to the Good Life." September 20, 2021. https://www.matthewkelly.com/post/the-secret-to-the-good-life.
21. Quote Investigator. "Quote Origin: I Do Not Know What I Think Until I read What I'm Writing." January 26, 2023. https://quoteinvestigator.com/2023/01/26/think-read/.
22. Wikipedia. "The medium is the message." Accessed March 29, 2025. https://en.wikipedia.org/wiki/The_medium_is_the_message.
23. Hor. Ep. 1.1.41– 42
24. Eldredge, Becky. "Ignatian Wisdom #11: Fixing our Desires." October 25, 2011. https://beckyeldredge.com/ignatian-wisdom-11-fixing-our-desires/.
25. Prov. 27:17 NIV
26. Mark 10:35-45
27. Yeats, W.B. *A Vision,* 220. United Kingdom: Palgrave Macmillan UK, 1959.
28. Matt. 13:24-30, 36-43
29. Penn Memory Center. "Bill Lyon's Battle with 'Al.' Accessed March 29, 2025. https://pennmemorycenter.org/news-events/bill-lyons-battle-al/.